The Stations

GW00362357

The Stations of the Cross

Caryll Houselander

Sheed and Ward
London

ACKNOWLEDGMENTS

The articles and prayers in this book first appeared in the American *Messenger of the Sacred Heart*, edited by Rev. Thomas Moore, S.J.

We wish also to thank Burns Oates and Washbourn, Ltd., for permission to use Mgr. Knox's translation of the Bible: and Mrs. Wyndham for lending the blocks from which the fourteen woodcuts by the author are reproduced.

CONTENTS

VIA CRUCIS

THREE o'clock on a grey afternoon. Outside, a steady drizzle of rain; inside the church, an odd motley of people.

A smartly dressed woman, side by side with one who is shabby and threadbare. A boy and girl who appear to be in love. A very old man, so bowed that he is permanently in an attitude of adoration. A stalwart young soldier whose polished buttons glitter like gems in the candlelight. A couple of students, shabbily but elegantly dressed in corduroys and bright scarves, rubbing shoulders with a gaunt, round-shouldered man who looks like a tramp. A sprinkle of small children; and behind them all, as if he felt himself to be the modern publican, though there is no reason why he should, a thick-set, square-shouldered business man. And, a few seconds before the priest, in come a couple of rather flustered little nuns, like birds shaking the rain off their black feathers.

What a diversity of places these people must have come from: luxury flats, tenements, small boarding-houses, institutions, barracks, studios, colleges, doss-houses, schools, offices, convents. What sharp contrasts there must be between their different lives and circumstances!

But they seem to be strangely at one here, gathered round a crude coloured picture on the wall of the Church, "The First Station of the Cross"; and it seems to come naturally to them to join together in the same prayer:

"We adore thee, O Christ, and we bless thee,
because by thy holy Cross thou hast redeemed the world."

The tender rhythmic prayer, that has been on the lips of men all through the ages, is repeated fourteen times as they move slowly around the church, following the priest from Station to Station, until they reach the last of all, "Jesus Laid in the Tomb".

An onlooker—one, that is, who was uninitiated—would be puzzled.

In between the repeated ejaculations, he would hear the priest reading meditations; at least he would hear the drone of his voice, but perhaps not what he said, as he would probably read without expression or punctuation. Even if he did hear the words, they would hardly be likely to enlighten him, for the meditations would, very likely, be couched in the most extravagant terms of sentimental piety, and seem to have no relationship to the stark reality of the human suffering which they attempted to describe.

Neither would the pictures on the wall help him to understand what it is that brings such incongruous, oddly assorted people together, in this seemingly formal and curious devotion. As likely as not the pictures would be uninspiring, crude, and without any aesthetic value.

If this onlooker asked one of the people there to enlighten him, she would probably be surprised that he should expect the pictures to attempt either aesthetic beauty, or to represent the physical aspects of the

Passion of Christ realistically. She might explain that the Church does not ask for pictures at all, but simply for fourteen numbered crosses marking fourteen incidents on the way to Calvary, showing not so much the exterior incidents of the Passion as their inward meaning.

She might add, with a shrug of the shoulders, that the Church tolerates the pictures that we use, just as a mother tolerates the crude and almost symbolic pictures that the older members of the family draw for the younger, knowing that the little children will read into them just those things which are already in their own hearts.

The Stations of the Cross are not given to us only to remind us of the historical Passion of Christ, but to show us what is happening now, and happening to each one of us.

Christ did not become man, only to lead his short life on earth (unimaginable mercy though that would have been), but to live each of *our* lives. He did not choose his Passion, only to suffer it in his own human nature, tremendous though that would have been, but in order to suffer it in the suffering of each one of his members, through all ages, until the end of time.

Most of Christ's earthly life was hidden. He was hidden in his Mother's womb, he was hidden in Egypt and in Nazareth. During his public life he was hidden often, when he fled into "a mountain to pray". During the forty days of his risen life, again and again he disappeared and hid himself from men. Today he is hidden in the Blessed Sacrament, in Heaven, and in his Mystical Body on earth.

But in his Passion he was exposed, made public property to the whole of mankind. The last time he went up into a mountain to pray, it was to pray out loud, in a voice that would echo down the ages, ringing in the ears of mankind for ever. It was to be stripped naked before the whole world, for ever, not only in body, but in mind and soul. To reveal not only the height and the depth and the breadth of his love for men, but its intimacy, its sensitivity, its humanity.

All his secrets were out. Every detail of his Passion revealed something more of his character as man. Not only his heroism and his majesty, but his human necessities, and the human limitations which he deliberately adopted as part of his plan of love, in order to be able to indwell us *as we are*, with *our* limitations and psychological as well as physical necessities and interdependence on one another.

He was not only simulating our humanness outwardly, but feeling as we feel. Not only feeling his *own* grief, fear, compassion, need of sympathy, and so on, as man, but *ours*. Not only knowing every nerve and fibre of his own love for us, but that of each one of us for one another.

The Passion of Christ was an experience which included in itself every experience, except sin, of every member of the human race.

If one may say this with reverence, the fourteen incidents of the Stations of the Cross show not only the suffering, but the psychology of Christ. Above all they show, in detail, his way of transforming suffering by love. He shows us, step by step, *how* that plan of love can be carried out by men, women and children to-day, both alone in the loneliness of their individual lives, and together in communion with one another.

Different though each human being is from every other, uniquely his own though each one's experience is, there are certain inevitable experiences which are common to all men and from which none can escape.

One of these is death. Another is love. Every human being alive is on the road to death. Every one is capable of love for *someone*, even if it is only for himself, and the price of love, perhaps particularly of self-love, is suffering. But the *power* of love, and this does not apply to self-love, is to transform suffering, to heal its inevitable wounds.

Now it is easier to understand what it is that brings the incongruous motley of people together to "make the way of the Cross".

Each one meets himself on the "Via Crucis", which is the road through death to life. In Christ he finds the meaning of his own suffering, the power of his own capacity for love. He finds the explanation of himself in Our Lady, the Mother of Christ. And in those others too, who are taking part in the Passion of the Son of Man—Simon of Cyrene, Magdalen and John, Veronica, the women of Jerusalem, the good thief, the centurion, the man who lent his tomb, the scattered apostles who crept back, and ran to the empty tomb on the morning of resurrection. Those in whom, through grace and mercy, Christ is being formed, and growing from the darkness of the buried seed to his full flowering.

Yes, in the Stations of the Cross, he who has the eye of faith sees the story of Christ's historical Passion— his own individual story—and the story of the suffering world, in which Christ's Passion goes on through time; the way of the Cross which, though it leads to the tomb and the dark sleep of death, leads on beyond it to the waking morning of resurrection and the everlasting springtime of life.

For us, here and now, there is a more immediate and more practical meaning in those fourteen incidents on the way to Calvary. It is a showing not simply of the way of sorrows, which we are all destined to walk, if we will or not, but of the way of love, which heals sorrow, and which we all can take if we walk in the footsteps Christ has marked out for us, and not only imitate him but identify ourselves with him.

The Stations show us how each one can lighten the heavy Cross that is laid upon the bent back of the whole human race now. Now each one in the power of Christ's love can sweeten his own suffering and that of those who are dear to him.

This is why the prayer "We adore thee, O Christ, and we bless thee, Because by thy holy Cross thou hast redeemed the world" echoes down the centuries, not in tones of fear and reluctance, but as a cry of welcome, a tender cry, in the tones of a lover's greeting, to him, whom every man must meet on the way of sorrows, changed for him to the way of love.

THE FIRST STATION: JESUS IS
CONDEMNED TO DEATH

"BEHOLD the Man!"
He is a man of sorrows. He is covered in bruises and stripes. He is made a laughing stock. He is crowned with a crown of thorns. A reed is put into his hand for a sceptre, a tattered soldier's cloak is thrown over his naked shoulders. His eyes are blind-folded. His face covered with spittings. He is bound like a dangerous criminal. His own people have chosen a murderer before him. His friends have forsaken him. The kiss of treason burns on his cheek.

"He has no comeliness whereby we shall desire him."

"He is a worm and no man, the reproach of men and the outcast of the people."

And he is condemned to death.

"Away with him!—Away with him!—Crucify him!"

"Behold the man!"

Behold the Son of God!

Behold the man abiding in mankind!

He has put on our humanity. He has put *you* on—and me. He has covered himself with our shame, blind-folded his eyes with our blindness, bound himself with our slavery to self. He is bruised by our falls. He bleeds from our wounds. He sheds our tears. He has made himself weak with our weakness. Faint with our faint-heartedness. He is going to die our death.

All men are condemned to die, but he is condemned to die not only his own death, but yours and mine, and that of every man whom he will indwell through all the ages to come.

"Behold the Son of God!"

"This is my beloved son in whom I am well pleased!"

He alone of all men born need not have died; but because things are as they are, because *we* have to pay the price of our sins, and our life on this earth must inevitably be a journey through suffering to death, Christ has chosen to give himself to every man who will receive him, so that each man who wills can tread that road with the feet of Christ, and at the end of it he can, if he wills, die, not his own death but Christ's.

That is why death is the choice of Divine Love.

"Dost thou doubt that if I call on my Father, even now, he will send more than twelve legions of angels to my side? But how, were it so, should the Scriptures be fulfilled, which have prophesied that all should be as it is?" (Matt. xxvi. 53–4).

His bound hands hold back the legions of angels.

He has chosen our impotence in order to give us the power of his love, our weakness to give us his strength, our fear to give us his courage, our ignominy to give us his majesty, our pain to give us his peace, our wounds to give us his power to heal, our dying to give us his life; our interdependence that *we* may give him to one another.

"Behold the man."

In him behold mankind!

Already in this mysterious moment of time, at the beginning of the Via Crucis, Christ has given himself to all those whom he will indwell through all the centuries to come; already he has taken them to himself, made them one with himself. All manner of men, and women, and children, the rich and the poor, the famous and the infamous, saints and sinners, all who will be redeemed by his Passion are in Christ, and his Heavenly Father sees them all as Christ, his Son in whom he is well pleased.

There, in the Prince of Peace, stripped and wearing a soldier's coat that has been put on him, are all the conscripts compelled to go to war. There in the young man in the flower of his manhood, going out willingly to be sacrificed, are all those young men who go *willingly* to die in battle for their fellow men.

"This is the greatest love a man can show, that he should lay down his life for his friends" (John xv. 13).

There, in the prisoner, bound, publicly shamed, condemned to the death of criminals, thieves, and murderers, are all the criminals who will repent, and accept death on the scaffold as their due.

There, in "Jesus of Nazareth King of the Jews", are the kings of this world.

"Art thou a king then?"

"It is thy own lips that have called me king."

"My kingdom is not of this world."

There, crowned with thorns, and bearing a reed for sceptre, are the kings of our days, whose crowns are thorn indeed and whose sceptres are reeds shaken by the wind.

There, in the blameless Lord, made subject to men, illimitably patient, silent when he is mocked, silent before Herod, silent when Peter denies him, are all those innocent children who are so commonly patient and inarticulate in suffering, and whose suffering and death baffles and scandalizes us.

". . . you will all be scandalized in me!"

There, in him, are the martyrs of all times; those of our own time with every detail of their martyrdom, including those which their persecutors try to hide, shown to the whole world.

The trickery—the utter injustice—the faked evidence—the verdict decided before the trial—and the things that have been done in secret to prepare the victim, if possible to break him: the mental torture, a veritable crowning with thorns; the long nights without sleep. Cruellest of all, the attempt to make him a stumbling block to his own people.

It is significant that everything contributing to that condemnation is parallel with everything that contributes to the passion of the martyrs of our own times.

The intrigues and the fears of politicians, the hatred of fanatics, mass hysteria. The unstable crowds swayed by paid agitators, the popular craving for sensation—and those many Pilates of our day, who wash their hands of the responsibility of knowing "What is truth?", who shut their eyes to Christ in man, and try to escape from their own uneasiness by evasions.

"I am innocent of the blood of this just man—look you to it!"

"In any case, there is nothing that *I* could do about it!"

Neither is it by chance that those who will carry out the sentence will be the young and ignorant soldiers of an army of occupation, lads brought up like the soldiers of the Red Army, deprived of the knowledge of the one God, obeying their orders without question, because they are conditioned to obey orders without questioning or thinking.

"Father, forgive them; they do not know what it is they are doing."

"Behold the man!"

Yes, and behold in him yourself. Each one of us can recognize himself, a sinner, in the disfiguring, the bruising, the ugliness, hiding the beauty of the fairest of the sons of men. And there can be few who do not recognize themselves too, in the utter loneliness of this man in the midst of the crowd that lately spread their garments to be trodden by the little ass he rode on, and now clamour for his blood.

"Behold we have seen him disfigured and without beauty; his aspect is gone from him; he has borne our sins, and suffers for us; and he was wounded for our iniquities, and by his stripes we are healed."

Prayer

"*Lord that I may see!*"
Give me light to see you in my even-Christian,
and to see my even-Christian in you.
Give me faith to recognize you
in those under my own roof.
In those who are with me, day after day,
on the way of the Cross.
Let me recognize you
not only in saints and martyrs,
in the innocence of children,
in the patience of old people
waiting quietly for death.
In the splendour of those
who die for their fellow men;
but let me also discern your beauty
through the ugliness of suffering for sin
that you have taken upon yourself.
Let me know you in the outcast,
the humiliated, the ridiculed, the shamed.
In the sinner who weeps for his sins.
Give me even the courage
to look at your Holy Face,
almost obliterated,
bruised and lacerated
by my own guilt,
and to see myself!

Look back at me, Lord,
through your tears,
with my own eyes,

and let me see you,
Jesus, condemned to death,
in myself,
and in all men
who are condemned to die.

THE SECOND STATION: JESUS RECEIVES HIS CROSS

They have put his own garments on him again, and Jesus comes out from the judgement hall of Pilate to receive his Cross.

He comes to it gladly! This is a strange thing, for the cross is a symbol of shame, and it is to be his death-bed. Already he sees the very shape of his death in the wide-spread arms. From this moment he will be inseparable from it, until he dies on it. He will labour and struggle under the weight of it until the end comes.

Yet, Christ welcomes the Cross. He embraces it, he takes it into his arms, as a man takes that which he loves into his arms. He lays his beautiful hands on it tenderly, those strong hands of a carpenter, that are so familiar with the touch of wood.

This is not the first time that Christ has welcomed the wood of the Cross. It is only the first time that he has embraced it publicly before the crowds. It is a tremendous gesture showing men his love for them openly, because this Cross which he is receiving is *their* cross, not his; he is making it his own for love of them, taking their cross, and lifting the dead weight of it from the back of mankind.

That is why Christ receives the Cross with joy and lays it to his heart. "Bear one another's burdens", he told men; now he takes the burden of the whole world upon himself.

Lying in the wooden manger in the stable of Bethlehem, Christ welcomed the Cross for which he had come into the world.

At the moment of his birth he accepted all the hardship, the pain and suffering of mankind. The cold, the darkness, hunger and thirst; the pain of mind and body, the needs and the dependence of all men.

He accepted death—indeed he became man in order to die for men.

Christ need not have suffered at all; he could have redeemed the world by a single breath drawn for His Father's glory, but he chose to take as his own the common suffering of all men. Unseen, unknown, Christ received his Cross in Bethlehem.

Long before he took hold of this great Cross in Jerusalem, he accepted it, and rejoiced in it. In the labours and hardships of all working men, he received his Cross as a boy in Nazareth. He welcomed and made his own the labours and necessities of all the workers who would come into the world. Like them he had to toil patiently, perseveringly, to acquire the skill for his craft, gradually to train his hands and his muscles and his mind.

Day after day, year after year, he, who had created the wood of the trees, wrestled with human limitations like other craftsmen, in order to be able to wrest the beauty from the wood, to show its flowing grain, its rose and ivory, its walnut and gold. To polish it with the smooth bright steel of his finely sharpened chisels.

In Nazareth Christ received his Cross. Working in the carpenter's shop he laid his hands upon it day after day, the wood that he was to glorify. He sawed and planed it, he drove the nails into it, and the joyous refrain that would be repeated again and again in the generations to come, was already the song in his heart:

> *"Faithful Cross, O tree all beauteous,*
> *Tree all peerless and divine!*
> *Not a grove on earth can show us*
> *Such a leaf and flower as thine.*
> *Sweet the nails, and sweet the wood,*
> *Laden with so sweet a load."*

He accepted the Cross in Nazareth, making the daily life of every worker his own; giving to the hardships, the monotony and the labours of countless hidden lives the power to redeem; restoring manual labour to the dignity of creative work, transforming it from being a punishment for sin, and only that, to a contemplation of God, in which the worker could know something of the joy of the Creator, in making that which he had conceived within himself.

If any man would come after me, Christ said, he must take up his cross daily. In Nazareth he took up the Cross of all working men daily.

Again, when he went out from Nazareth into the wilderness to "begin to be tempted by the devil", and from thence to the cities and villages to do his Father's will, he took the common suffering of all men to himself —temptation, privation, weariness, hunger and thirst, separation from those dear to him, misunderstanding from friends, frustration.

Now, with his love gathering to its climax, he accepts the heaviest cross of all, which every man born must accept, the certainty of his death.

This is the shadow which falls across the light in the springtime of life, the shadow of the Cross, which Christ welcomes now at the beginning of the Via Dolorosa. Taking it to his heart, he takes all those who fear death to his heart; all those who must face the knowledge of a painful illness which can have but one end; all those who wait without hope of reprieve for a death sentence to be carried out on them by other men; all those old people haunted by the certainty that their days are numbered.

Look at this Cross, so much bigger than the man whose body will be stretched to fit it. So much higher than the height of the man who will be lifted up above the earth on it, and who being lifted up will draw all men to himself.

Christ receives it with joy because he knows that this is the dead weight that must have crushed mankind had he not lifted it from their backs. This is the dead wood, which at his touch is transformed to a living tree. At his touch the hewn tree takes root again, and the roots thrust down into the earth, and the tree breaks into flower.

Already in Bethlehem, when the new-born child lay in the manger, a secret bud shone on the tree of life; now it is going to break into flower for ever, and that flower will sow the seeds of life that will never die, for Christ is the flower and the seed.

Because Christ is to be stretched to the size of the Cross, all those who love him will grow to the size of it—not only to the size of man's suffering, which is bigger than man, but to the size of Christ's love that is bigger than all suffering.

Because Christ is to be lifted up on the Cross, all those who love him will be lifted up above the world by the world's sorrow; because he being lifted up will draw all men to himself, they will draw all men to him in themselves.

Because Christ has changed death to life, and suffering to redemption, the suffering of those who love him will be a communion between them. All that hidden daily suffering that seems insignificant will be redeeming the world, it will be healing the wounds of the world. The acceptance of pain, of old age, of the fear of death, and of death, will be our gift of Christ's love to one another. Our gift of Christ's life to one another.

No man's cross is laid upon him for himself alone, but for the healing of the whole world, for the mutual comforting and sweetening of sorrow, for the giving of joy and supernatural life to one another. For Christ receives our cross that we may receive his.

Receiving this cross, the cross of the whole world made his, we receive *him*; he gives us his hands to take hold of it, his power to make it a redeeming thing, a blessed thing, his life to cause it to flower, his heart to enable us to rejoice in accepting our own and one another's burdens.

"If any man has a mind to come my way, let him renounce self and take up his cross and follow me. The man who tries to save his life shall lose it. It is the man who loses his life for my sake that will secure it."

Prayer

Lord!
let me receive the cross gladly,
let me recognize your cross in mine,
and that of the whole world in yours.

Do not let me shut my eyes
to the magnitude of the world's sorrow,
or to the suffering of those nearest to me.
Do not let me shrink from accepting my share
in that which is too big for me,
and do not let me fail in sympathy
for that which seems trivial.

Let me realize
that because you have made my suffering yours,
and given it the power of your love,
it can reach everyone, everywhere.
Those in my own home,
those who seem to be out of my reach.
Can reach them all
with your healing, and your love.

Let me always remember
that those sufferings
known only to myself,
which seem to be without purpose
and without meaning,
are part of your plan
to redeem the world.

Make me patient
to bear the burdens
of those nearest at hand.
To welcome inconvenience for them,
frustration because of them.
Let me accept their temperament,
as they are,
nurse them in sickness,
share with them in poverty,
enter into their sorrows with them.

Teach me to accept myself—
my own temperament,
my temptations,
my limitations,
my failures,
the humiliation of being myself, as I am.

Allow me, Lord,
all my life long,
to accept both small suffering
and great suffering,
certain that both
through your love
are redeeming the world.

And in communion with all men,
and above all with you,
let me accept joyfully
Death.
And the fear of death—
my death
and the deaths of those whom I love.

Not with my will
but with yours,
knowing that you
have changed sorrow to joy,
and that you have changed
death to life.

THE THIRD STATION: JESUS FALLS
THE FIRST TIME

A T THE very first step of the way to Calvary, Jesus stumbles and falls. He is down on his knees in the dirt!

What has happened to this man? this man who had just now declared himself to be King of a spiritual world, with legions of angels at his command; who has been known to hold back the overwhelming force of the storm and still the raging seas by an act of his will; who by a mere touch of his hand caused a living fig tree to wither, and has fallen now under the purely material weight of the Cross he so lately welcomed!

Only a few moments ago he held out his arms to receive it, seemingly with joy; now at the very first shock of its weight on his shoulder he has fallen.

The crowd thronging outside the judgement hall are laughing derisively; some of them remember hearing him say that *any* man who wanted to follow him could only do so, carrying his cross: now it seems that *he* can't even take the first step on the way to be marked out by his footprints without falling!

Is not this the man who claimed to be the Son of God? Why, he is not even a superman, he is not even equal in stamina to one of those splendid young Roman soldiers who are prodding him with their spears to get up. After all he is just an ordinary man, like any other in that huge crowd milling around him!

Yes, Christ is living through the experience of *ordinary* men, of each and every ordinary man in whom he will abide through all the ages to come.

He has not come into the world to indwell only exceptional men, or supermen; he is not here and suffering his Passion in order to be glorified in those who succeed where others fail, or to make himself an exception to ordinary men; he has come to live out the life of every man, of *any* man who has *any* love for him at all and tries to keep his word.

"If a man has any love for me, he will be true to my word; and then he will win my Father's love, and we will both come to him, and make our continual abode with him" (John xiv. 23).

The Cross which Christ has fallen under is the cross that most ordinary men fall under, and that at the beginning of adult life; a material cross, the burden of the material struggle that nearly everyone must shoulder.

This is the first fall, the first fall that each one of us knows. With the shock of it and the shame, Jesus takes the shock and the shame for us all.

There in him we are watching ourselves today. There is the young man or woman taken by surprise by the violence of the first sudden onslaught of the temptations of grown-up life. There is the one who a little while ago, from the dream world of adolescence, welcomed the hardships and struggle of economic life in a spirit of adventure, tripped up by the first stumbling block of the materialism of the real world. There is that one who imagined that natural love alone could sustain him in marriage on a pinching wage, flung down by the first impact of grinding poverty, for himself and his bride. There too is that most broken-hearted one who, in a land of martyrs, believed he could accept suffering and dreamed of martyrdom for himself, but at the first shock of the terrible reality, the first hard, rough crushing of the cross on his own back, has fallen—an ordinary man, persecuted by the supermen of the ideologies, derided and mocked by his own disillusioned fellow countrymen.

Yes, Christ, prostrate there under the Cross, lives through the humiliation and bewilderment of those who seem to fail at the start. Those taken suddenly and by surprise, who came out full of self-confidence to wrestle with and overcome the world, to overcome its materialism, its political and economic systems, its injustice, its hardships and its terrors, confident that they could set their feet in Christ's footsteps, shoulder his Cross, and make the journey of life, only to find themselves tripped up in his first footprint.

"And they have stretched out cords for a snare for my feet; they have laid for me a stumbling block by the wayside!"

That prophecy was spoken of Christ, of Christ fallen under the Cross in Jerusalem, of Christ living on in all who are cast down by the grief and humiliation of the first fall.

He, who never yielded to temptation himself, has already lived through and overcome the discouragement and the sorrow of those who do.

That is why Christ chose to be, not a superman, not in a physical sense an extraordinary man, but an ordinary man.

He allowed his own words about the majority of those who would follow him, to be in a sense applicable to himself.

"The spirit is willing but the flesh is weak."

We did not identify ourselves with Christ, he identified himself with us.

It is humiliation, wounded vanity, that makes it difficult to get up and go on after the shock of the first fall.

If we have failed before others, if we have fallen openly, making ourselves objects of contempt and derision, it is still more difficult; our humiliation is the more bitter because we have not only betrayed ourselves *to* ourselves, but we have made fools of ourselves before men. They will watch us now, they know our weakness, they will watch our "heroics" as we try to start again, and they will mock at us!

Christ, who chose to be an ordinary man on the Via Crucis, chose to feel as ordinary men feel. Foretelling the anguish of his Passion, it was the mockery that he spoke about first of all—"the Son of Man shall be mocked and spat upon and crucified".

Because Christ identifies himself with us, because *he* suffers the humiliation of the first fall in us, his love transforms it. The very wound can heal us.

The first fall is the first real self-knowledge. Now we know our weakness, we know our helplessness before the difficulties of life, our total inability to shoulder our responsibilities. We know that we cannot get up by ourselves, we cannot shoulder the burden for the second time by ourselves, we cannot face our own self-contempt or the derision of ourselves by others.

We realise now that we are wholly dependent on Christ, dependent on him to act in us, to lift himself up in us, and to lift us up in him.

His weakness is our strength.

In the light of this new self-knowledge, in the realization and acceptance of our utter dependence on him, the second start, look as it may before men, is infinitely better in the eyes of God than the first.

No longer do we seek to carry the burden with our own hands, but with his.

No longer do we try to walk in his footsteps, we tread the way with his feet.

Prayer

Lord
We thank you
for your compassion for us,
for the mercy of your first fall
under the Cross.

We thank you
because you have identified yourself
with us,
who are ordinary, weak men and women.
You have made yourself one
with those who fail,
who are humiliated,
who are overcome by circumstances,
those who fall at the beginning of the way.

We thank you
because you fell
at the beginning of the way to Calvary
for us.
Fell for us, under the material weight
of the hewn wood.

You carried the burden—
the heaviness of our circumstances,
the load of material things.
You accepted the difficulties
that sometimes overwhelm
each one of us.
You took to yourself

*the painful humiliation
of our first fall.*

*You gave us your weakness
to be our strength.*

*Grant to us, Lord,
that the shock of the first sin,
of the first failure,
at the beginning of life
may give us self-knowledge
and a truer knowledge of you.
May help us to know ourselves
and you,
and to know the depths of your love.
May it teach us
our dependence on you,
and that without you
we can do nothing.*

*Turn the humiliation
caused by our vanity
into your humility,
and lift us up in your power
and with your courage
to take the cross
and to start again on the way,
trusting now,
not in ourselves
but in you.*

THE FOURTH STATION: JESUS MEETS HIS MOTHER

JESUS is on his feet again, the Cross is put back on his shoulder, once more he starts on his way. As he lifts his bowed head and looks at the road he is to tread, he comes face to face with his Mother.

It is not by chance that she meets him at this moment, just as he falls and struggles to his feet again.

She sees that which no one else in that crowd sees— the tiny child, taking his first unsteady steps and falling on the garden path in Nazareth.

She is there beside him, holding her breath, longing to put out her hands to hold him, to prevent the fall, but she lets him go alone, the little child whose independence she must respect, her son who must learn to walk on his own feet, and to walk away from her.

For his Mother those first steps of the baby learning to walk were the first steps on the road to Calvary.

The "Word was made flesh"—*her* flesh. God had taken human nature, *her* human nature.

The way of the Cross had begun. Already his face was set steadfastly towards Jerusalem.

It was for this journey that she had fashioned those blameless feet from her own flesh and blood.

Seeing the first fall on the Via Crucis, his Mother sees the first fall on the path in Nazareth. Now as then she is silent, she holds back her hands as she did then. His

will is her will. It was for this hour that she gave him
to the world, for this that he grew from the infant to the
child, from the child to the man.

He goes on his way. He passes her by: this is something at the very heart of his suffering, that it must
afflict her whom he loves; that because they both love,
neither can spare the other. He goes on his way, to do
his Father's will.

"And now my soul is distressed. What am I to say?
I will say, Father save me from undergoing this hour of
trial; and yet I have only reached this hour of trial that
I might undergo it" (John xii. 27).

But why—why? The unvoiced cry in the soul of the
Mother of Jesus is the cry of every woman who sees her
child suffer or die, and every woman sees her innocent
child in the grown man.

Mary is identified with every woman to come who
must be separated from her child by his pain, his
sorrow, his death, his impotence to spare her, her
impotence to save him.

Standing there, while Christ passes her by, she is
every woman who must stand aside while her son goes
to war. She is every woman who knows that her child
is to die on the scaffold. She is every woman whose
child is a failure, covered in shame and loved only by
his mother. She is every mother who must sit, with
heart constricted, by the bedside of her dying child—
strangling that cry in her throat, that question hammer-
ing on the drained-out brain: "Why—why—why—
should innocence suffer this thing, why should this one
in the flower of his manhood be sacrificed, why should
this child whom I love bear the shame and grief of the
whole world?"

Mary asked the question long ago, asked for all the mothers yet to be.

"My Son, why hast thou treated us so?"

Down the years echoes the voice of the answering child, "Did you not know that I must be about my Father's business?"

What is his Father's business but the business of love, the Father's love for mankind? "The Father so loved the world, that he gave up his only son to save the world."

The Father so loved men because each one of them in his eternal decree was to be identified with Christ, his beloved Son, to be given Christ's own life to be his. Had there been no sin, everyone whom God created would have been "a Christ": each one a glorious expression of God's love, living with Christ's life.

Christ is given to save the world.

Mary has given him the precious blood that is to be shed. It is to be shed in order that it may become the blood stream that is the life of every man who lives in Christ, the blood stream of the Mystical Body of Christ on earth through all time, the life blood of the world flowing through the heart of humanity.

When Mary uttered her "Fiat"—"Be it done to me according to thy word"—when she conceived Christ and gave him her own humanity, she made every mother to come a potential Mother of Christ, every child who would come into this world, one who was to come to be a Christ to it.

"If anyone does the will of my Father who is in Heaven, he is my brother and sister and mother."

Every woman who sees her child suffer, every woman who is separated from her child. Every woman who must stand by helpless and see her child die, every woman who echoes the old cry "Why, why, why *my* child?" has the answer from the Mother of Christ.

She can look at the child through Mary's eyes, she can know the answer with Mary's mind, she can accept the suffering with Mary's will, she can love Christ in her child with Mary's heart—because Mary has made *her* a Mother of Christ. It is Christ who suffers in her child; it is his innocence redeeming the world, his love saving the world. He too is about his Father's business, the business of love.

Suffering is the price of love. The hardest thing, but the inevitable thing in the suffering of every individual, is that he must inflict his own suffering on those who love him.

It is love that redeems, love that can heal the world, love that can save it.

Suffering has no power in itself; it is only powerful to save when it is caused by love, and when it is the expression of love.

The Mother of Christ loved the world with *his* love. She gave him to the world for the love of those whom he loved, those who would be born into the world generations hence, those among whom are you and I. Witness the lyrical song of her love for us, ringing down the centuries from the first Advent:

"Behold, from this day forward all generations will count me blessed."

She rejoiced because her child was to bring joy into the world, was to flood the world with his love.

The cause of Christ's suffering was his love for the world, the suffering he gave to his Mother was the gift of his own love. The increase of Christ's own grief

because he must afflict her, was an increase of Christ-
love in the whole world—the suffering which is a communion of love.

Compassion, the communion in suffering of those who
love, is the suffering that redeems; it is Christ's love in
the world; it exists only because people love one
another, and because it exists it begets more love.

Christ goes on his way; no word is spoken now; Mary
follows him in the crowd. Another woman has anointed
his feet for his burial; another will meet him on the way
and wipe the blood and dirt from his face; others will
weep aloud for him.

Mary remains silent; she does not lift a hand; only
when he is suffering no more will she anoint his body.
She simply accepts this supreme gift of his love, his
suffering given to her.

It is a complete communion with him. They are as
completely one now as they were when he was the child
in her womb, and her heart-beat was the beating of his
heart.

Prayer

Mother of Christ,
Help me to be willing
to accept the suffering
that is the condition of love.

Help me to accept
the grief
of seeing those whom I love
suffer,
and when they die
let me share in their death
by compassion.

Give me the faith
that knows Christ
in them,
and knows that his love
is the key
to the mystery of suffering.

Help me,
Blessed Mother,
to see with your eyes,
to think with your mind,
to accept with your will.

Help me to believe
that it is Christ
who suffers in innocent children,
in those who die in the flower of manhood,

in those whose death is an act
of reparation,
in those who are sacrificed
for others.

Remind me
that their suffering
is Christ's love
healing the world,
and when I suffer for them
and with them
I, too, am given the power
of his redeeming love.

THE FIFTH STATION: SIMON HELPS
JESUS TO CARRY HIS CROSS

JESUS has come face to face with his Mother and gone on his way.

Now his Mother is following him as one of the crowd. How often she, who of all people is dear to him, has been among the crowd following him, glad even to catch a glimpse of him and to hear his voice in the distance!

He is labouring under the Cross. It is too much for him to carry alone. Everyone can see that, but no one offers to help him.

Someone then must be forced. The soldiers seize upon Simon of Cyrene. It has, or he thinks it has, nothing to do with him. He was simply about his own business in Jerusalem; it seems to him mere chance that he met this tragic procession—an unlucky chance for him, but there it is! He is made to take up the load and help this man, a stranger to him, and whom he supposes to be a criminal on the way to his execution.

Really there is no chance in the incident; it is something planned by God from eternity—to show men the *way* of Christ's love.

"I am the way, the truth, and the life."

It means that no one is meant to suffer alone. No one is meant to carry his own cross without some other human being to help him.

Again Christ is proving to the world that he has come

to live the life of all ordinary men on the simplest human terms.

Now, as he accepts the reluctant help of Simon, accepts it because he perforce *must*, and yet, in his humility, gratefully, he is showing each one of us whom he will indwell, what he asks of us and what he wants us to give to one another.

A man who claims to be self-sufficient and not to need any other man's help in hardship and suffering has no part in Christ.

The pride which claims to be independent of human sympathy and practical help from others is unchristian.

We are here to help one another, we are here to help Christ in one another.

We are here to help Christ blindly; we must know him by faith, not by vision.

We must help him not only in those who seem to be Christlike, but more in those in whom Christ is hidden: in the most unlikely people, in those whom the world condemns. It is in them that Christ, indwelling man, suffers most; it is in them he cannot carry his Cross today without the help of other men.

Simon of Cyrene saw only three criminals (of whom Christ was one) on the way to die. He could not know, until he had taken up that stranger's Cross, that in it was the secret of his own salvation.

Simon thought, at first, that Christ was no business of his. He did not even know him. He did not seem to be worth helping; his own interrupted business in Jerusalem that day seemed much more important to him.

Why should he put his own business aside, why give his strength, his time, and even his suffering for this

man? He must have suffered; the hard heavy wood
would have torn and blistered his hands, or if one end
of the Cross was laid on his shoulders it would have
bruised it as it bruised Christ's: the way to Calvary
must have been exhausting, and have sapped the energy
he wanted for his own affairs. Again, he must have
suffered mentally; the frustration of his own plans, perhaps those on which very much depended, and the
humiliation of being ordered to do this thing by the
hated Roman soldiers, bits of boys anyway, who found
it amusing to inconvenience and make mock of a
Jew!

We must be ready to carry the burden of *anyone* whom
we meet on our way, and who clearly needs help—not
only those who "deserve", or seem to "deserve", help.

Everyone is our "business", and Christ in every one,
potentially or actually, has a first claim on us, a claim
that comes before all else.

We are here on earth to help to carry the Cross of
Christ, the Christ hidden in other men, and to help in
whatever way we can. We may, like Simon, have,
literally, a strong arm to give; we may help to do hard
work, we may have material goods to give; we may have
time, which we desperately want for ourselves, but
which we must sacrifice for Christ in man; we may have
only suffering. Suffering is the most precious coin of
all: suffering of body, suffering of mind, paid down
willingly for Christ in man, enables him to carry his
redeeming Cross through the world to the end of time.

Suffering contains in itself all that Simon gave—our
mind and body, frustration, and identification with
someone else: that last is the germ of our own salvation,
the way to transform the self-pity that is the danger in

all suffering, to the love of other people which reaches out a hand to Christ, and saves us.

We do not look for Christ only in saints; we look for him, perceive him by faith, and try to help him, most of all in sinners. It is in sinners that Christ suffers most to-day, in them that his need is most urgent.

St. Thérèse of Lisieux, the most innocent of saints, prayed as a child for a condemned and unrepentant murderer awaiting execution. The man repented and died in the grace of God. The child Thérèse was Simon carrying Christ's Cross.

We need not—indeed must not—wait to be saints or even to be "good" to help Christ to carry his Cross.

Christ *asked* for help, for sympathy in his Passion; he accepted whatever anyone would give him—*anyone*—not those who were already saints!

He asked the three apostles, of whom Peter was one, for sympathy in Gethsemene: he did not ask them to do anything to avert his suffering, but only to be with him in it, to share it with him through compassion. "Could you not watch one hour with me?"

They were willing but weak, they failed him then, though later, when he again asked help from them, they gave it and were sanctified. Christ did not turn from them because they failed him in his hour of need. To Peter he entrusted his Church, to John his Mother, and James was allowed to die for him. He was grateful for the tender compassion of Mary Magdalene, the woman who was a sinner; he accepted the gift of precious ointment poured out over his feet—he accepted it with pathetic gratitude. "When she poured this ointment over my body, she did it to prepare me for my burial;

and I promise you, in whatever part of the world this Gospel is preached, the story of what she has done shall be told in its place, to preserve her memory" (Matt. xxvi. 12–13).

He accepted the unwilling help of Simon of Cyrene —the grudging help of those who are forced to serve, or give against their will, to those in whom they have little interest; those who to-day are conscripts, compelled to serve for others; or those forced, sometimes by human respect, to help tiresome friends or relations in whom they have no interest; he accepted the help of Simon who was half-ashamed to help him, as to-day in the condemned and outcast and the "unworthy" he accepts the help of those who make themselves absurd in charity, those who are "exploited", "taken in", made "fools for Christ's sake".

Christ, who identified himself with sinners, who hid his beauty under the ugliness of sin, turned to sinners as much as to saints for help, both material and psychological help. Here is the extreme proof of the strong realism of his love for men.

He was grateful for the help of the thief on the Cross, the generosity of this derelict dying man, who acknowledged Christ's goodness, when those who knew him well had fled and others derided him: he was grateful to this broken sinner who acknowledged him with his last breath—"This day you shall be with me in Paradise."

Even when he was dead, he accepted his tomb, the place where his body should rest, from Nicodemus, the hesitating, careful man, who wanted wistfully to follow him, but dared only to come to him under cover of darkness.

There is no exemption from the love of Christ in one another, or from sharing the cross.

There is no moment when, if we meet one whose burden is too heavy, we may delay in helping to carry it.

It is not for those who are good alone to help Christ; it is most of all for sinners, for the weak, the hesitating, even the selfish, to force themselves to take up the cross; and, in the cross of Christ, even those who seem to be lost find salvation and joy.

Every day, hidden under our sins, abject in his need, Christ says to the sinners who put out a hand or speak a word to help him, "This day shall you be with me in Paradise!"

Prayer

Lord,
give us faith
to know you
in your direct needs,
in your uttermost loneliness,
bearing your heaviest load,
and unable to bear it alone,
in the most unlikely people.
In those who do not look like you,
who do not speak like you,
who perhaps do not even know you
though you are suffering in them.

Give us patience
and fortitude
to put Self aside
for you,
in the most unlikely people.
To know that every man's
and any man's suffering
is our own first business,
for which we must be willing
to go out of our way
and to leave our own interests.
Give us,
most humble Saviour,
the humility to forget ourselves
and even our sinfulness,
so that we may never allow
consciousness of our own unworthiness

to prevent us from helping you
in any man
whom we meet on the way
in need.

Give us the wisdom
that knows that there is no sanctity
excepting in love
and the living of love.

THE SIXTH STATION: VERONICA WIPES THE FACE OF JESUS

Now, WHILE Simon labours under the Cross with Jesus, while Mary, his Mother, follows behind him in the crowd, someone—a woman—forces her way through the rabble, even through the guard of Roman soldiers surrounding him, and comes face to face with Christ. She is driven by compassion.

The face that the Lord turns to her is terrible to look on; it is difficult to believe that it is the face of the Son of God. It is difficult even for those who have once seen his face shining with the brilliance of a fire of snow upon Tabor, to believe in him now. Two of them have fled from him, just as those others have done though they have seen him command the wind and the waves and raise the dead.

Now that face of infinite majesty and compelling beauty is unrecognizable. The eyes which could see into the secret places of men's souls are blinded, swollen from the long sleepless nights of trials and judgement, and filled with sweat and blood. The cheeks are bruised and dirty; the mouth swollen; the hair "like ripe corn" is tangled by the crown of thorns, and matted with blood.

Certainly there is no sign now of the beauty that could win a man's heart by a single glance, or of the power that can rule the tempests and give life to the dead.

On the contrary, here is a man who is the very personification of humiliation, who is ugly with wounds

and suffering, who is in the hands of other men who
have bound him and are leading him out to die, and
who is not even able to carry his own Cross alone.

It is all this, from which his close friends have fled,
which drives this woman to him. It is the ugliness and
the helplessness which frightened those whom he called
his "own" away, that draws her to him; it is her compassion that gives her the courage to come close to
him.

She comes with a veil in her hands, a cloth on which
to wipe the poor, disfigured face.

She kneels, as we kneel to wipe the tears from the
faces of little children. Gratefully, the head bowing
over her sinks into the clean linen cloth, and for a brief
moment is covered by it.

Then he raises his head and she, kneeling there, her
own face lifted, sees the face of Christ looking down at
her, and behind it the great beam of the Cross. The
two are together within the shadow of the Cross on the
street, Veronica and Christ.

She sees the majesty that was hidden, for now she has
wiped away what she can of the blood and sweat and
tears; she sees that they hid a face that is serene in its
suffering, calm, majestic, infinitely tender. The swollen
mouth smiles; the exhausted eyes are full of gentleness;
the expression, after all, is not one of defeat and despair,
but of triumph and joy.

The power of Christ is able to control fiercer storms
than those of the wind and the sea. It is able to still the
torrents of evil of the whole world in the stillness of his
own heart. It is the power which enables him to
command the floods of all the sorrow in the world and
hold them within his peace. It is the power which can

not only give life back to the dead, but can change death itself to life. It is the power of divine love.

So, for a moment, a vision more wonderful than that of Tabor is granted to the woman whose compassion drove her to discover Christ in a suffering man. Then Christ passes on, on the way of sorrows, leaving her with the veil in her hands and on it the imprint of that face of suffering that hid the beauty of God.

In Christ burying his face in that woman's veil on the Via Crucis, we are looking at the many children of to-day whom war has twisted and tortured out of the pattern of childhood, who are already seared and vitiated by fear, persecution, homelessness and hunger.

We see grown-up people who have been maimed or disfigured, those whom chronic illness or infirmity has embittered. We see, too, those most tragic ones among old people, those who are not loved and are not wanted by their own, those in whom the ugliness, not the beauty, of old age is visible. We see the tragic ones who are cut off from all but the very few, the Veronicas of the world, by mental illness. We see, too, many who are dying, who with Christ are coming to the end of their Via Crucis, yet sometimes without realising that Christ is suffering for and in them.

Suffering is not something to sentimentalise. It can obliterate even the beauty of childhood. It can ennoble but it can also degrade; it can enlarge a man's heart, but it can also contract and shrink it. To the sufferer who does not know that he is indwelt by Christ, his pain of mind and body, his humiliation and loneliness, are baffling. He can see no purpose in it; he is embittered by it, and his bitterness sets up a barrier between himself and others, imprisoning him in his own loneliness. Outwardly, he shows only the ugliness of the world's sorrow, suffering and all the effects of sin.

It is the Veronicas of to-day who wipe away his ugliness from the face of Christ living on in man. The Veronicas of to-day are all those in whom compassion overcomes fear and repulsion, all those who seek and find the lost and the forsaken, the downtrodden and the lonely. Those who seek the maladjusted, broken children of our wars and our slums, who go on their knees to wipe the tears from their eyes.

They are the nurses who comfort the dying in hospitals, who wipe the sweat of death from their faces. They are the Sisters of Mercy who go into the homes of the sick and poor to serve them. They are all those who befriend the friendless in our mental hospitals. They are those who, in their own families, tend and comfort the old and infirm in their last days.

They are, too, those priests who minister to the dying, and who go into the prisons to absolve the prisoners and restore Christ in their souls; those priests who follow men to the scaffold, cleansing them with the spiritual waters of absolution.

It is not only the physical wounds that the Veronicas of to-day tend and cleanse; it is, by that same act of tender compassion, the mental and spiritual wounds, the emotional wounds that corrode and fester in the spirit, almost obliterating the image and likeness of Christ. It is not only the sweat that blinds the eyes of the dying that they wipe away, but that which blinds the soul. Ignorance of Christ, ignorance of their own supreme destiny of being "other Christs", misunderstanding of suffering and its ugliness, that ugliness so resented by those who cannot see beneath it.

Until someone comes to reveal the secret of Christ indwelling the sufferer's soul to him, he cannot see any purpose in his pain. There is only one way to reveal Christ living on in the human heart to those who are ignorant concerning it. That is Veronica's way, through showing Christ's love. When one comes, maybe a stranger, maybe one close at home but whose compassion was not guessed before, and reveals Christ's own pity in themselves, the hard crust that has contracted the sufferer's heart melts away and, looking into the gentle face of this Veronica of to-day, the sufferer looks, as it were, into a mirror in which he sees the beauty of Christ reflected at last from his own soul.

Until Veronica came to him on his way to Calvary, Christ was blinded by blood and sweat and tears. The merciful hands of Veronica wiped the blindness from his eyes; looking into her face, he saw his own beauty reflected in it. He saw his own eyes looking back at him from hers. She had done this thing in the power in which alone she *could* do it, the power of Christ's own love.

In the compassion on her lifted face, Christ saw, in the hour of his extreme dereliction, the triumph of his own love for men. He saw his love, radiant, triumphant in her, and in all the Veronicas to come through all time—in them and in those sufferers in whom his own divine beauty would be restored by their compassion.

Prayer

Saviour of the world,
take my heart
which shrinks
from the stark realism
and ugliness of suffering,
and expand it with your love.
Open it wide
with the fire of your love,
as a rose is opened
by the heat of the sun.

Drive me by the strength
of your tenderness
to come close to human pain.
Give me hands
that are hardened
by pity,
that will dip into any water
and bathe any wound
in mercy.

Give me your hands,
hands that heal the blind
by their touch,
hands that raise the dead
and are nailed to the Cross;
Give me your hands
to tend the wounds of the body
and the wounds of the mind.

Give me your eyes
to discern the beauty of your face
hidden under the world's sorrow.
Give me the grace
to be a Veronica,
to wipe away
the ugliness of sin
from the human face,
and to see
your smile on the mouth of pain,
your majesty on the face of dereliction
and, in the bound and helpless,
the power of your infinite love.

Lord, take my heart
and give me yours.

THE SEVENTH STATION: JESUS FALLS
THE SECOND TIME

HARDLY has Veronica wiped the dirt from his face than Christ is down in the dust again: he has again fallen under the heavy load of the Cross. How different it is in reality to the picture on the wall! There Christ seems rather to be genuflecting under the Cross than falling under it; he bows his head, certainly, but hardly a hair is out of place; his robes, the snowy white tunic and the scarlet cloak, are still clean and are not torn.

The reality, that which happened two thousand years ago, and the reality which happens in the lives of those in whom Christ lives to-day, is not like that. Christ is thrown down on to the ground, his face in the dust; he is unable to get up until others come forward to heave the Cross up from off his back, and perhaps help him to his feet again. It is yet another example of how Christ makes himself need the help of others to redeem the world.

They do not know that they are unwittingly taking part in the redemption, those young Roman soldiers who pull the Cross from Christ's prostrate body and help him to his feet.

They are carrying out the day's work, obeying orders blindly. It is their business to see that death does not cheat them of their victim until they have dealt with him in the way they are commanded to; until they have crucified him.

It is only because it happens to be Jesus Christ whom they are lifting up and helping to his feet again: Jesus Christ whom they are loading with the Cross once more for the last stretch of the road: only because it is Jesus Christ that, all unknowingly, they are taking a part in the redemption of the world.

To-day, the young soldiers of the ideologies unknowingly take their part in the world's redemption, carrying out their orders to keep their prisoners alive for so long as it suits their masters, when they drive them along the desolate roads to exile and ultimately to death. They too take part in the redemption when their prisoners are those in whom Christ lives—"other Christs" in whom his Passion is being lived out.

Likewise those warders and executioners who must support criminals who are condemned to death, criminals who have purified their souls by contrition and go gladly to the death that expiates their sin, they too, all unknowing, through the heavy, sordid duty they carry out, play a part in the world's redemption.

Christ is down in the dust—this second fall is harder than the first; he is nearer the end of his tether now, more dependent than before on others to help him to get up and go on. It may have been something trifling, almost absurd, that threw him down. Perhaps something as small as a pebble on the road; yes, that would have been enough to send him hurtling down, with that terrible burden on his back, and his own exhaustion as he nears the end of his bitter journey.

It is the same to-day, the same for those "other Christs" who have gone a long way on the road and who fall, not for the first time now, under the heavy cross of circumstance—those who have carried this cross for a long time, who have become exhausted by the unequal struggle, and fall; who, with him, are down in the dust.

It is for them that Christ falls for the second time and lies under the crushing weight of his Cross, waiting for those who will come forward to lend their hands to lift it from his back, and enable him to go on to the end of his way of suffering and love.

The crushing weight of circumstances to-day, the economic conditions, make the Christian life a cross, which, even though it is a redeeming cross, is hard to carry. The weight of public opinion, the contempt for those who choose the hard way because it is Christ's way, the weight of material hardship, the weight that grows heavier and heavier as those who must carry it come nearer and nearer to the end of the journey, the weight of the cross, the sheer material weight that was heavy enough to throw Christ down, to throw God face down in the dust. If something as trifling as a pebble in the road or a false step could throw Christ down on the road, so may a tiny provocation, a sudden temptation, a mocking word, a fragment that adds to the struggle, bring the man staggering under the cross down. The servant is not greater than his master.

It is not only soldiers and warders under orders who can lift the cross from Christ's back to-day, not only they who can help Christ to his feet again. Everyone who labours to lift the burden of material misery from the backs of the poor, gives his hands to free Christ from the crushing burden.

Everyone who concerns himself to change public opinion and to make the Christ life honoured in the world, helps Christ to his feet again.

Everyone who forces his way against the indifferent mob, against the unthinking multitude who see nothing but folly in Christ and his Cross, helps to drag back the great burden from his exhausted body.

Everyone who approaches Christ fallen under the Cross, coming to him in friendship and love, to relieve him of the burden of the Christian life lived in isolation and loneliness, in opposition to the whole modern environment, helps Christ to his feet in the world again, and sets him on his way.

Everyone who recognizes *who* it is that has fallen there, *who* it is for whom the burden of circumstances, of materialism, of temptation, has proved too persistent and too heavy, lends his hands to lift the Cross from the prostrate Christ, and to set Christ on his way to the consummation of his love once more.

Prayer

Jesus Christ,
exhausted on the long road
to Calvary,
fallen for the second time
under the weight of the Cross.
Allow me to be among those
who come forward
out of the crowd,
to heave back
the great load
that crushes you,
in my even-Christian.

Do not let my hands
or my mind
or my heart
be idle,
or indifferent to
or unaware of
the conditions of life,
the difficulties
and problems
facing those
who struggle against heavy odds
to live the Christ life,
and to share in the work
of your love.

Grant that I may never
disassociate myself from you

in the Christian
who has fallen under the burden
of your Cross.
Who, worn out
by the struggle
against temptation,
against circumstances,
against public opinion,
and the opinions of his own people,
is down in the dust,
crushed by the burden
of humiliation,
failure
and shame.

Give me grace
to help to lift you up
in that man.
To set him on his feet,
to help him on his way
on the road you have trodden.
And when I fall
send me those
who will lend their hands
to lift my burden,
and enable me too
to follow you
to Calvary.

THE EIGHTH STATION: JESUS SPEAKS TO THE WOMEN OF JERUSALEM

Now Christ is followed by a great multitude of people, among them women who mourn over him, who weep aloud for him.

A strange thing happens: he turns to them and says, "It is not for me that you should weep, daughters of Jerusalem; you should weep for yourselves and for your children."

Strange, because at first sight it seems that he, who accepts every straw of compassion with pathetic gratitude, refuses the brave, open compassion of these women!

It is, or seems to be, a contradiction; it is not like him to refuse anything from anyone.

We have seen how, until now, and indeed all through his Passion, he has accepted the compassion of anyone at all who would give it to him—accepting even the forced help of Simon. But this accepting on Christ's part began long before the hour of his Passion struck; it was part of his plan of love from all eternity, his plan to depend on his creatures, to need them, to need all that they could and would give to him to fulfil that unimaginable plan of his love.

First of all he depended on Mary, his Mother. Before he was born he was in this world among the men and women and children whom he had come to save, but hidden from them in her. He could go only to where she carried him, he could only speak through her words, his heart beat only through the beating of her heart.

From the very beginning he asked for the simple substances that his own creatures could give him, to use to do the work of his love and redemption in the world. He asked Mary for her flesh and blood, for her self.

In Bethlehem he accepted even what the animals could give him. With the same love with which he accepts the wooden Cross on this culminating day of his Passion, he accepted the wooden manger that the humble beasts could give him; he was stretched on that at his birth as he will be stretched on the Cross in his death. He was grateful for the animals' straw, for their warm clover-sweet breath on his tiny limbs.

He accepted the homage and the gifts of the poor shepherds, and the gold, frankincense and myrrh of the wise men—strange gifts for a little new-born child, perhaps even an embarrassment to St. Joseph, who might have been suspected of theft were they found on him, a poor artisan, when he had fled into hiding in Egypt.

Grown to manhood, Jesus still asks for simple things, whatever his creatures can give him to use in working his miracles; especially miracles of multiplication, symbols of his self-giving to all men. In Cana, he asks for cold water, cold water to be changed into the rich life-giving wine.

In the wilderness, he accepts the seemingly absurd little gift of a few loaves and small fishes from a boy in the crowd, to be changed into food to feed the whole multitude.

To preach the Word, to give the message of his Father's love, he borrowed Peter's little fishing boat, just as he would borrow another man's tomb when his love was consummated.

But above all else it is compassion that Christ has always wanted from men, has always asked for; he has wanted them to be with him, to comfort him just by entering into his suffering with him—not to take away his suffering but to enter into it with him, because it is *his* and it is the expression of his love for them.

What then is the meaning of this curious refusal of the compassion, of the tears, of the women of Jerusalem?

"It is not for me that you should weep, daughters of Jerusalem; you should weep for yourselves and for your children. . . ."

Is this a refusal, a rebuke, or a warning?

In a sense it is none of these, but a showing, a pointing to something which, if these women miss, and if *we* miss to-day, they and we will have missed the meaning of Christ's Passion. Which, if we miss, all our devotion to the person of Jesus Christ in his historical Passion, all our meditations and prayers, will be sterile, and will fall short of their object to reach and comfort the heart of Christ.

He is pointing to his Passion in the soul of each of those women, in the soul of each of their children and their children's children all through time.

He is pointing to all those lives to come through all the ages in which his suffering will go on.

For himself the consummation of his love for the world is close: he is very near to Calvary now; in a few hours it will be over, he will be at peace and he will have entered into his glory; but in the souls of men his suffering will begin again, and it will go on all through the years to come.

Evil will go on gathering strength all through the centuries to come; the Christ in man will be assaulted and threatened by it.

There will be many who will follow literally in Christ's footsteps—who will enter into his glory with him through his sacrifice. Martyrs who give their life for their faith, young men who willingly give their life for their country, children who die Christ's own redeeming death, because they die in the full power and splendour of innocence.

It is not for these that we must weep, though we may weep for ourselves in our seeming loss of them; they are the privileged ones whose love is immediately consummated in Christ's love.

We must weep for ourselves and for our fellows, in whom Christ suffers on, still labouring, stumbling, falling on the Via Crucis, still mocked and goaded and assaulted on the way, still in the midst of the struggle.

There are those in every age in whom the suffering Christ is manifest, almost visible, the beauty of his love shining through the ugliness of their circumstances: it is not for Christ in them that we must weep. It is for Christ whose beauty is hidden, Christ in the outcast, in the man who is wrestling with temptation, who is unrecognized, uncomforted; Christ in those whom we pass by without seeing, without knowing, whom we allow to stagger on his way, loaded with his too heavy Cross, unhelped, unwept, uncomforted.

It is in order that we should seek him and give our compassion to him, weep for him in these, that Christ showed his need for sympathy in his earthly life and on the way of the Cross.

We must weep for him in these and in our own souls,
in these days, the days of the dry wood—"It is not for
me that you should weep . . . you should weep for
yourselves and for your children. Behold a time is
coming when men will say, it is well for the barren, for
the wombs that never bore children, and the breasts that
never suckled them. It is then that they will begin to
say to the mountains, Fall on us, and to the hills,
Cover us. If it goes so hard with the tree that is still
green, what will become of the tree that is already
dried up?"

Prayer

Father,
do not let me find consolation
in sensible devotion
to the person of Jesus Christ,
while Jesus Christ passes me by
unrecognized,
unknown,
unsought,
uncomforted
on the Via Crucis
we travel together.
Do not let my heart
be moved by pity
for the painted Christ on the wall,
while it remains a stone,
hard, insensitive
to Christ suffering alone
in the ugliness
of shame and disgrace,
in the outcast,
the shunned,
the forgotten,
in mental sufferers
hidden away in hospitals,
in prisoners serving life sentences,
in people wrestling with bitterness
and despair behind the Iron Curtain,
in those fighting a losing fight
with human weakness and degradation—
in the unhelped,

the uncomforted,
the unloved.

Do not give me tears
to shed at the feet
of the Crucifix,
while they blind me
to Christ crucified,
unwept for
in the souls of sinners
and in my own
sinful soul.

THE NINTH STATION: JESUS FALLS THE
THIRD TIME

AT LAST the pitiful procession has reached the foot of
Calvary. Once more Christ is to go up into a
mountain, this time for the last time.

Here he is at last, at the end of the Via Crucis, at the
foot of the mountain; and with him Simon of Cyrene,
the stranger who is sharing the weight of his Cross; the
two thieves who were led out with him, one on each
side; and, surrounding them, holding the crowds back
with their spears, and goading the condemned men to
the last lap, the steep climb up the hillside, the soldiers
of the Army of Occupation, unwittingly playing their
mysterious part in the redemption of the world, by
carrying out what is for them simply routine duty,
obeying orders without question to-day, as on every
other day.

Behind them, held back by the spears, the spears that
ring the defenceless Lord, is Mary his Mother, Mary
Magdalene, and the other holy women who followed
him and his apostles about the cities when he went
about preaching and healing all manner of diseases.
With them the boy John, the boy singled out by Christ
as the object of his particular love.

And there is a great multitude following—the multitude that have thronged the way from the Judgement
Hall.

There are those sensation-mongers, who have come
out of morbid curiosity—the same who stand outside

the prison gates to see the black flag go up on the morning of an execution; those who sat round the guillotine during the French Revolution, or who crowd round a street accident, not to help, but to gloat.

There are those who have been healed by Christ—those who were lame, who could not have followed, pushing their way through the rabble, but for his touch; those who were lepers; perhaps even some whom he, who is about to die, has raised from the dead.

There are flocks of poor people, destitutes and beggars, those who heard him promising them a kingdom, promising that if they followed him they should be clothed in more than the glory of Solomon, that they should be fed and that they should never thirst—that they should possess the earth. To what do they follow him now, these the bewildered and disillusioned poor?

Where is the kingdom that they were promised?—and what has become of their King? One of the young soldiers carries a notice in his hand: he has stuck it on to his spear; everyone can see it—"Jesus of Nazareth, King of the Jews". It is written by Pontius Pilate's own hand, the hated Roman Governor who is mocking them through mocking their King.

There are others following him, those women of Jerusalem who wept for him, others too who have wept for him, who believe in his innocence: perhaps he has been foolish, but certainly he has never been wicked: certainly he did not try to stir the people to sedition, on the contrary he seemed to try to make them content with conditions that they, the Jews, had always revolted against, to be content to be poor, to be humble, to be meek, even to "render to Caesar the things that are

Caesar's". Yes, certainly the man is baffling, but he is not wicked and he is not seditious. They remember how humble he was himself, and how kind; how he took their children into his arms and embraced them and blessed them. They weep for him.

And there are those who follow him because they hate him and fear him. Because they are still afraid that somehow he may escape from them; before now he has been known to disappear from the midst of a dense crowd; it is not impossible that he may do so again. He has been known to work miracles; it is not impossible that he will work one now, on his own behalf. So those who hate and fear him follow him hoping to see the end of him, unwilling to let him out of their sight.

As they approach the foot of Mount Calvary the suspense reaches its climax. If he is going to work a miracle he must do it now; if he is going to show that after all he *is* what he claims to be, the Son of God, the moment has come for him to prove it.

It is not only those who fear and hate him who are in suspense; the whole multitude watches him, holding its breath, waiting to see what Jesus of Nazareth is going to do now.

The morbidly curious are hoping now for a final sensation; they want as it were their "money's worth". They can follow criminals to execution practically any day; *this* promises to be a special event.

Those who have been healed, who have been raised from the dead, those who weep for him, those whose children he has lifted in his arms and blessed, strain forward, hoping against hope that he whom they still believe in, still believe to be innocent, will, at the eleventh hour, vindicate their faith, will show the triumph of goodness over evil. Surely this pure, guileless, flawless man must prove that goodness and honesty are more powerful than intrigue, corruption and petty politics?

As for the poor, the vast majority in that swarming, jostling crowd, they push themselves forward, struggling to be in the front of the crowd, waiting, praying, crying out for the miracle that will give them their triumph, their kingdom after all!

What will he do? now that he has come to the foot of Calvary, and the little cavalcade has paused to push the Cross more securely on the man's shoulders, while he braces himself for the ascent. It is his last chance to show that he is a king, that he is the Son of God. Will he suddenly straighten himself up and turn to vanquish his enemies by the sheer majesty and power flashed off from him, will he summon legions of angels to his defence and scatter the soldiers and those who are hostile in the crowd? Will he even speak to them with the old majesty, the old authority, piercing them to the heart by his words, as he did on that other mountainside long ago?

They wait, straining forward, struggling to come near to him, breathless with suspense, some through fear, some through hope, all tense, expectant, waiting.

And what does he do? For the third and the last time, Jesus falls under the Cross.

This is the worst fall of all. It comes at the worst moment of all. It tears open all the wounds in his body; the shock dispels the last ounce of strength that he had mustered to go on, it shatters the last hope, the last remnant of faith in nearly everyone in the crowd.

It is triumph for his enemies. Heartbreak for his friends.

The effect on the crowd is terrible. From having been an object of compassion, of admiration, he has become an object of contempt. Hope has given way to despair, struggling faith to bitterness and derision— "He has saved others, himself he cannot save!"

Now Christ gets up; he does not turn his head, he does not heed the disappointment of the crowd. He gets up, weaker than he has ever been, almost too exhausted to go on, all the old wounds open and bleeding: more abject than he has ever been, a greater disappointment to his followers than he has ever been—in their eyes a complete failure. He gets up and goes on, lays his beautiful hands, those hands of a carpenter, on the wood of the Cross for the last time, and without looking round begins the ascent to the summit of Calvary.

The last fall is the worst fall; in it Christ identified himself with those who fall again and again, and who get up again and again and go on—those who even after the struggle of a lifetime fall when the end is in sight. Those who in this last fall lose the respect of many of their fellow men, but those who overcome their humiliation and shame, who, ridiculous in the eyes of men, are beautiful in the eyes of God, because in Christ, with Christ's courage, in his heroism, they get up and go on, climbing the hill of Calvary.

In the third fall, the showing of Christ's love is this: he does not indwell only the virtuous, only those who are successful in overcoming temptation, only those who are strong, and in whom his power is made manifest to the world; he chooses to indwell those who seem to fail, those who fall again and again, those who seem to be overcome, even when the end is in sight.

In them, if they will it, he abides; in them he overcomes weakness and failure; in them he triumphs; and in his power they can persevere to the end, abject before men, but glorious with Christ's glory before God.

Prayer

Lord,
fallen under the Cross
for the last time,
grant to me and to all those
with whom you identified yourself
in the third fall,
your courage,
your humility:
to rise in your strength
and, in spite of failure upon failure,
shame upon shame,
to persevere to the end.

Do not let us despair.
Let us go on in your power,
when those who believed
in your presence in us
are disillusioned.
When those who sought you
in our lives
are scandalized
and have lost hope in you
because of our failures.
Give us courage
to go on, in your name,
even when your enemies
discredit you
because of us.

Let us rise in your strength
even in this extremity,

when we are alone before God,
and he alone knows
your presence still abiding in us;
because in your third and last fall
under the Cross,
in the sight of God and men,
you identified yourself with us.

THE TENTH STATION: JESUS IS STRIPPED OF HIS GARMENTS

ONCE MORE Jesus has been helped to his feet, in order that he may suffer to the end.

Once more the Cross has been put upon his shoulders and he struggles on, still dragging it up to the summit of Calvary.

All around him, filling his ears, filling his mind, half deafening him, the cries of the crowd break over him like the waves of a sea in storm. A sea in which it would seem impossible not to be drowned.

They are cries of derision, of hatred, of disappointment, of despair, despair with a note of accusation against him; cries of contempt; cries which could and would drown the soul of any man who loved less than he loves, who knows less of human nature than he knows.

These people who are disillusioned, disappointed, contemptuous, even these people who fear and hate him, are those whom he loves and who, when at last he has dragged the Cross to the summit of the hill and been lifted upon it, will be drawn to him.

And not only will *they* be drawn to him, but their children, and their children's children, all through the generations to come.

Drawn to him, not only because he is their King, and because his love is manifest in his dying for them—"This is the greatest love a man can show, that he should lay down his life for his friends" (John xv. 13)

—but drawn to him, too, because each one of them will discover themselves in him.

All through the ages to come men will turn to the crucifix, and each one will see himself and his own particular suffering in the suffering of Christ on the Cross. They will see their own suffering in his, and laid upon him their own individual sins; and him triumphant in his love, turning their suffering to their glory and redeeming their sins.

If, instead of the third fall at the foot of Calvary, with all its seeming failure and shame, Christ had turned his back upon Calvary, healed his own wounds by a miracle, and vanquished his enemies, men would have feared him for all time, but they would not have loved him.

But in his physical weakness as a human being, in his struggle to the Cross, and on the Cross, Christ identified himself with all the weak and sinful men in the ages to come, who would be healed by his wounds.

"And I, if I be lifted up, will draw all men to me."

But before he is nailed to the Cross, Jesus gives us yet another overwhelming showing of his love, yet another proof of his identification with men in their bitterest humiliations.

Jesus is stripped of his garments.

It is hard to bring oneself to reflect on this, yet it is necessary because of what every detail of this dreadful incident can mean to men to-day.

With all the wounds on his body—the wounds of the scourging, of the falls on the way to Calvary, of the heaviness and the roughness of the Cross on his shoulder —Christ's garments must have been stiff with blood and adhering to his body. The soldiers would not have treated him tenderly, although there is no reason to suppose that they were fundamentally cruel. They would undoubtedly have torn his clothes from him, as quickly as they could, and as roughly as they must. It would have been almost as if his skin was being torn off him.

There, exposed in his nakedness, he stood in front of the whole mob, and—which must have been far harder to bear—in front of those whom he loved, his Mother, John his chosen friend, and Mary Magdalene who had washed his feet with her tears, he stood naked.

He was stripped there on the summit of Calvary, not to reveal his Sacred Body in its perfection. He was the fairest of the sons of men; no other man had ever had, or ever would have, a body approaching his in perfection; but it was exposed to the world only when it was disfigured by wounds and bruises, only when it was exhausted and almost falling to the ground with weariness.

Again Christ identified himself with those whom he would indwell through all time.

He stood there naked in front of the world and in front of his Heavenly Father identified with all those sinners who are found out, whose shame is made public, or, perhaps more terrible for them, shown to those whom they love and from whom above all others they would wish to keep it secret.

He stood there identified with the neurotic who wants to hide his secrets under the thin disguise of his neurosis, and whose secrets are torn from him by modern "scientific" treatment.

He stood there identified with the convert either from sin or from unbelief, who must tear off the long established habits of sin and weakness, as if he were tearing off his skin.

He stood there identified with everyone who loves, because everyone who loves must be known sooner or later as he is, without pretence, his soul stripped bare in its nakedness.

Not long ago Christ had revealed his glory upon a mountain. He had gone up with his disciples to Mount Tabor, and there shown them his splendour, clothed in garments of burning snow: now he has gone up into a mountain again to reveal yet another glory that is his, the glory that he gives to sinful men in the hour that seems to them to be their hour of shame, but which, when it is identified with him, stripped naked upon Calvary, is an hour of splendour and redemption.

There in Christ is the sinner who is found out, the lover who is stripped of all pretence, the weak man who is known for what he is, the repentant murderer who pays the price of his sin willingly before the world, the child whose disgrace is known to the mother whom he wanted to make proud of him, the friend who is stripped of all pretence before the friend from whom he longed for respect.

There upon Calvary Christ's love for the world is shown in its nakedness, his love for the sinner in its intensity.

What became of Christ's garments, precious relics that they were, soaked with his blood, worn to his shape, to the shape of his body, the shape of his life and his labours?

To-day we have not so much as a thread that was woven into his garments, just as we have not even a shaving like a rose petal, picked up from the floor of

Joseph's workshop in Nazareth—let alone a chair or a table made by the Son of God.

"The soldiers when they had crucified Jesus took up his garments, which they divided into four shares, one share for each soldier. They took up his cloak, too, which was without seam, woven from the top throughout; so they said to one another, Better not to tear it; let us cast lots to decide whose it shall be. This was in fulfilment of the passage in Scripture which says, They divide my spoils among them; cast lots for my clothing" (John xix. 23–4).

We were meant to have more than relics of Christ. We were meant to have, and *are* meant to have, Christ himself.

If his garments had been preserved, they would have been relics to draw pilgrims from all over the world, only to kneel in front of them, perhaps to kiss the reliquary that contained them.

Christ meant something much more than that for us. Just as, when he was stripped of his garments, he put on the nakedness of our shame, we were meant by him to put *him* on like a garment, to put on the shape, the purity, of his body, the shape of his labours, of his human nature, his sleeping and eating and journeying, his austerities and his delights in the good and beautiful things of creation.

We do not know the story of the soldier who won Christ's seamless garment in the lottery. It is good to think that even in that tragic hour on Calvary, those boys, who were the Roman soldiers who crucified Christ, were stayed by their sense of what was beautiful and good from destroying the cloak that was woven in one piece.

Certainly the soldier who won it would never have destroyed it, he would have worn it himself; he who without fault of his own helped to crucify Christ was the first to "put on Christ", to try to fit his own body to the shape of Christ—the forerunner of us all, who must put on Christ, who must try to grow to his stature, to the shape of his labours, his purity, his majesty, his humanity.

Who must try, and this is the most profound and the most difficult thing of all, to grow towards the shape and pattern of his love, his love for men that accepted even their shame as if it were his own.

Prayer

Jesus,
Stripped of your garments
upon Calvary,
give me the courage
and the humility,
to be stripped before the world
of all pretence.
To show myself,
even to that one whom I love
and whose good opinion of me
is vital to my happiness,
just as I am,
naked,
stripped of everything
that could hide
the truth of my soul,
the truth of myself from them.

Give me
your own courage,
your humility,
your independence,
which compelled you,
for love of me,
to stand on that hill
of Calvary,
naked,
covered in wounds,
without comeliness
whereby we could know you.

Give me the courage
and the dignity and splendour
of your love,
to live openly,
without pretence,
even when there is that in my life
which shames me.
Give me the one glory
of those who are disgraced
and ashamed before the world,
to be stripped with you,
Jesus Christ,
my redeemer,
upon Calvary.

THE ELEVENTH STATION: JESUS IS NAILED TO THE CROSS

THERE was an hour of terrible darkness at the beginning of his Passion, when Christ was overwhelmed by the anticipation of the suffering he was to go through, when the vision of the evil for which he was to bear the shame overwhelmed him, and the utter loneliness in which he must face and accept the anguish of spirit that seemed to be beyond human endurance crushed him to the ground. Those whom he loved, for whom he was going to accept this dreadful suffering and death, could not stay awake to share his anguish with him, to give him at least even the support of their sympathy.

Three times on the way to Calvary his body failed him; even that tremendous will of love which enabled him to accept the Passion after his prayer in Gethsemene could not wholly overcome the weakness of his human body struggling on under the Cross. He had to be lifted to his feet, he had to be helped by a stranger.

But now, though many generations will pass before men see this clearly, now that the Passion is coming to its climax, Jesus is no longer afraid; he no longer asks to be spared; on the contrary, by his own will he is crucified, by his own will he is nailed to the Cross, fastened to it in such a way that he cannot come down, cannot fall from the Cross.

He who is God is also man, perfectly man; he will not allow any miracle to help him now.

He who is going to indwell every man who loves him, be he sinner or saint, through all the generations to come, accepts the limitations of their human nature as his own, and so that he may not *fall* from the Cross, by his own will he lets himself be fastened to it.

His human mind is tranquil now; no fear overwhelms him; his suffering, his dying, is made acceptable to him by love.

He is thinking now of other men, of those who are crucifying him; and he is thinking of them, praying for them, in words that everyone can hear clearly, words of unimaginable love and pity: "And when they reached the place which is named after a skull, they crucified him there; and also the two criminals, one on his right and the other on his left. Jesus meanwhile was saying, Father, forgive them; they do not know what it is they are doing" (Luke xxiii. 33–4).

To those who stood around, the majesty of Christ's prayer and of his acceptance of the crucifixion was not obvious. It was something wholly outside their comprehension; this incredible triumph of his love seemed to them to be simply the endorsement of his failure.

They could not believe that if he really had supernatural power, he would let things come to this; that if he was really King of the Jews and had come to save them and establish his own kingdom, he could allow himself to be actually fastened on to the Cross to die.

This was not conquering the world; this, at best and worst, was forsaking the world, escaping from the world, giving up the fight!

But still, even now there is the possibility that he may save himself—and them—by a miracle, a miracle that will stagger their enemies and conquer the world for himself, and for them.

"The people stood by, watching; and the rulers joined them in pouring scorn on him; He saved others, they said; if he is the Christ, God's chosen, let him save himself. The soldiers, too, mocked him, when they came and offered him vinegar, by saying, If thou art the King of the Jews, save thyself" (Luke xxiii. 35–7).

To those who stood by it must indeed have seemed now that Christ was separated from other men; he had been led out, outside the city wall, to die; he was rejected by his own chosen people, he was powerless in the hands of those who must crucify him almost without interest, in the course of their ordinary duty. He was an object of mockery and scorn; he seemed to be a fool, and as a fool his enemies treated him; as a fool, or perhaps a madman, they thought of him now. Even those who loved him were abashed and silent; his Mother alone was silent because she entered perfectly into his suffering with him. There was no need for any words between Jesus and Mary. His Passion was hers —her silence his; but others were silent with dismay, with fear, even with doubt and disillusionment—the thing was beyond words now; a word of loyalty to Christ, a word of pity, would have been enough to endanger a man's life; at the very least it would have made a fool of him too.

That was how things *seemed* to be, but in reality, as Christ stretched out his beautiful craftsman's hands and composed his blameless feet on the hard wood of the Cross to receive the nails, he was reaching out to countless men through all time; as he stretched his body on that great tree that was to flower with his life for ever, he gave himself to be made one with all those who, in every generation to come, would willingly bind and fasten themselves irrevocably to the cross, for the love of God and the love of men.

For all through time, for those who love Christ and who want to be one with him, Love and the Cross would be inseparable; but because Christ willed that he should be nailed to the Cross himself in his human nature, love will always predominate and redeem the suffering of the Cross.

As the three nails were driven home into the wood, fastening him to it irrevocably, Christ gave himself to all those men and women who in the years to come would nail themselves to his Cross by the three vows of religion—poverty, chastity and obedience: those wise ones who know the weakness of human nature, who know how easily the will can falter when the sweetness of the first consolation of prayer is over; how hard and bleak the winter of the spirit when its springtide and its summer and harvesting seems past for ever; how hard to go on faithfully clinging to the Christ-life with only one's own weak will to drive one; Christ receiving the nails gave himself to those men and women who would nail themselves by binding vows to himself upon the Cross, who would have the ability to remain true to their chosen life because their hands and feet are put into his hands and feet and they are held on to the Cross by the nails that held him.

He gave himself in that moment to all those men and women who would pledge themselves to him and to one another with the vows in matrimony, the blessed nails of human love safeguarding husbands and wives from the assaults of temptation in every circumstance of the world.

He gave himself to all those converts who bind themselves to the laws of the Church, and all those Catholics who persevere in the Faith, nailed to it by their own baptismal vows no matter what hardships it may involve them in, nailed to it willingly because they know well that without Christ they can do nothing, and that Christ in this world is inseparable from his Cross.

And with what great tenderness, with what depths of understanding Christ gave himself in that hour on Calvary to all those whom he would indwell—Religious, married people, ordinary Catholics, trying to adhere to him, not through emotion, not through sentimentality, but by uniting their wills to his, and binding themselves irrevocably to him. With what love he gave himself to them, knowing how they too would be considered to be fools, would be mocked and even looked upon with distrust and anxiety by their own people—by those who loved them.

He reached out in that moment to those who by entering religion would give scandal, as he himself was doing: "This night you will all be scandalised because of me."

They would be derided as he was derided; he would be derided in them: "You are escapists."

"You are giving up the fight."

"You are afraid of responsibility."

"You are afraid of life."

And this, despite the fact that in many countries of the world to-day, openly to vow yourself to religion is to put your head into the noose, to invite persecution.

Not only would the Religious be thought to be fools, but those married men and women who were faithful and compelled themselves to be faithful to their vows— whose love and whose fidelity to love is not that which the world of to-day can understand.

"What?" their mockers would say in the twentieth century. "What?—you are faithful to that man or that woman whom you are tired of, you deny this other man or woman whom you love passionately! How can you believe that a God who *is* love asks this of you?" Or to the man and wife who deny themselves for their children: "How can you be such fools? Surely you do not think that a good God can wish you to have children who will be poor, who may even have to grow up as labouring men, as his own Son did! How can you bring children into the world to be poor, to live hard lives, perhaps to go to war and to lay down their lives for their friends?"

And to the seemingly insignificant faithful Catholic, who is neither a Religious nor married, but who clings to the Faith, adheres to it firmly with a will that is grounded and rooted in the will of Christ: "What fools you must be and how abject! How can you, in these days of enlightenment, of free thought, of new ideas, of raw philosophies, accept dogma and doctrine? How can you allow your *minds* to be ruled by the Church?"

And even the sentimentalists who profess to love God and who love to be moved to feelings of tenderness and sweetness by sermons and the singing of hymns, exclaim scandalized: "How *can* you go to church because you *must* and not because you feel like it? How can you believe what you are told to believe and not what you *feel* to be true?"

To all these Christ reached out across the years when he was nailed to the Cross; he identified himself with them, he accepted their limitations, he gave them his will; for them as well as for himself, his prayer was uttered for ever. "Father, not my will but thy will be done."

Prayer

Lord,
wholly surrendered
to the will of your Father
and wholly identified with us,
Lord, nailed to the Cross
by your own choosing,
teach us to obey,
to accept,
to bow to the will of God.

Give us the wisdom
and the strength
to pledge ourselves,
to bind ourselves irrevocably
to the Law of your Love.
Let us so bind ourselves
that we will not only
adhere to you
in times of consolation,
in times of sweetness and devotion,
and when life goes smoothly,
but yet more securely
in the bleak and bitter
seasons of the soul—
in the hard iron of the winters
of the spirit.

THE TWELFTH STATION: JESUS
DIES ON THE CROSS

AT LAST the road to Calvary is trodden and now it
lies behind Jesus, who has gone up the mountain-side for the last time, and been stripped of
his garments and lifted up on the Cross.

Now from the Cross, before his eyes are darkened, he
can look back down that road which is indeed an
image of the road through life of all those who will come
after him.

On that road he has known those things which every
Christian, every one who follows him, must know too
on the journey between birth and death.

He has known pain, exhaustion, apparent failure,
shame; but it has not only been tragedy. He has known
too the blessed dependence of a man upon other men,
he has been helped by them and accepted their help,
he has realized the joy and the light that comes to other
men through helping him, above all through helping
him to carry his Cross; he has known compassion from
the women he met on the way, compassion and the
heroism that it inspires—the women who blessed him
openly with loud voices and Veronica who dared the
mockery of the crowd and the authority of the armed
guard to come close to him and wipe the tears and the
filth from his face.

On that road too he has seen the absolute triumph of
his Mother's love and trust for him and for his Heavenly
Father; she has not doubted him, against all human

reason she has believed in him; on that road where so much was dereliction and shame, her "Fiat"—"Be it done to me according to thy word"—has flowered with unimaginable splendour. His Passion is her Passion. She has followed him all the way, and, by her side, the beloved disciple John, the boy who is to take the place of Christ as her son. And, immensely comforting to him, Mary Magdalene, the notorious sinner who dared the censoriousness of the Pharisees, has now dared the mob surging about him on the Via Crucis, and followed him to Calvary. With her, other loyal heroic women, who are with him now beside the Cross: ". . . his Mother and his Mother's sister, Mary the wife of Cleophas, and Mary Magdalen, had taken their stand beside the Cross of Jesus. And Jesus, seeing his Mother there, and the disciple, too, whom he loved, standing by, said to his Mother, 'Woman, this is thy son.' Then he said to the disciple, 'This is thy Mother.' And from that hour the disciple took her into his own keeping."

To his enemies this seems to be the hour of their triumph and Christ's defeat, but in fact it is the supreme hour of *his* triumph. Now, when he seems to be more helpless than he has ever been before, he is, in fact, more powerful. When he seems to be more limited, more restricted, his love is boundless, his reach across the world to the hearts of men in all ages is infinite.

But to those who look on, how different what appears to be happening seems to what is really happening.

How certain it seems that Christ has been overcome. That his plan of love for the world has failed utterly, that he himself is a failure. His "kingdom" a pitiful delusion.

Can this be the same Christ who only three short

years ago went up into another mountain and spoke to the multitudes, filling the heart of each individually with secret joy and hope? Teaching the poor their own glory, revealing the secret of his personal beatitude to each one who suffered, to each who was down-trodden or unjustly treated, showing them each the reality of the poetry of life, the inwardness of the kingdom which was already theirs if they could receive it with simplicity and the values of unspoilt children?

Did he not tell them, and did they not believe, that their very poverty clothed them not in drab worn garments but in those that, seen by the true vision, are richer than Solomon's robes? Lovelier than the iridescent lilies growing in the fields of Palestine?

Did he not convince them that if their hearts were pure, the Kingdom of Heaven was already theirs, and he himself who strewed the wild flowers under their feet and gave them the morning star, their King?

But now on this other mountain-side how different everything seems to be! What hope is there now for them? Their King is poorer than any of them, he is stripped of all that he has, his crown is a ridiculous crown of thorns, he has nothing left of his own, not even a grave to receive his dead body; far from being clothed in splendour that rivals the glory of Solomon, or beauty that rivals the wild flowers, his own natural beauty is hidden under wounds and bruises.

"He has no comeliness whereby men shall know him."

Even as a little infant in Bethlehem, he has never seemed so helpless as he seems now.

The hands that could raise the dead to life with a touch, could heal the sick and give sight to the blind, are nailed to the hard wood: immovable, stiffening in death. The feet that blessed the delicate grass by their touch, that walked on the swiftly moving waves of the storm at sea, are fastened down to the rough trunk and held still. The eyes that could see into the depths of the soul are darkening with the blindness of death.

The tongue that spoke the words of eternal love is swollen with thirst, and stiffened in death. The heart of the man who is love itself is turning to a small hard stone that a man could hold in his hand.

More bitter than all his other suffering is the desolation of his soul, his own unutterable loneliness, the sense of being wholly unsupported by any love, emptied out, forsaken even by God—"and at the ninth hour, Jesus cried out with a loud voice, Eloi, Eloi, lama sabachthani? which means, My God, My God, why hast thou forsaken me?" (Mark xv. 34).

He seemed to be quite alone, quite defeated, dying a useless death at the end of a useless life, the tragic life of a poor deluded dreamer, who, because of his fondest delusion, that his love for the world could save it, had come to a still more tragic death, to die alone, an object only of scorn or pity—not even hated now, since now he is powerless—beaten. Men hate only when they fear.

"The passers-by blasphemed against him, tossing their heads; Come now, they said, thou who wouldst destroy the temple and build it up in three days, rescue thyself; come down from that Cross, if thou art the Son of God."

But Christ would not come down from the Cross. "I, if I be lifted up," he had said, "will draw all men to me." Now he had done just that, he had drawn all men to him because he was dying all of their deaths for them, he was giving himself to them in death, so that in their turn they would die his death, with his courage, his love, his power to redeem.

From that moment when he bowed his head crying out, "Father, into thy hands I commend my spirit", and died, everyone indwelt by him to the end of time would die his death, with his power to heal and strengthen and redeem themselves and other men, by their dying.

He came to the tremendous mystery of his death alone; he felt forsaken even by God; but from that moment until the end of time, no Christian man or woman or child will die alone. Each one will die Christ's death, their hands in his hands, their feet folded upon his feet, the last beat of their hearts the beat of his heart; and because he has made their deaths his own, theirs too will have the power of his to save themselves and those whom they love.

There are people who are haunted all through their lives by the fear of death, and when it comes close—when it is no longer something far away, which they cannot even imagine happening to themselves—it is a hard thing to accept, let alone to welcome or want.

Most of us are too weak, too sinful and too much unaware of the other world to long for God as some of the saints do. We are far too rooted in earthly things, too dependent for the flicker of courage that we have upon creatures and creature comforts.

We do not, we cannot, realise that we are going into the light and the warmth: that in God we will find again everyone and everything that we loved here—and more than that, because the most lovable of his creatures is only the very dimmest reflection of himself.

We not only cannot realise the light and warmth that we are going to, but we feel ourselves slipping into silence and darkness. We want to cling to people, to hear their voices, to see their familiar faces, to feel the comforting touch of their hands. We want to cling for ever to the here and now that we know, and suddenly the here and now is slipping away from us, and we can no longer hold on to it.

After all, it seems now that death is near that we do not know God the Father at all. Of course, long ago we made countless acts of love, but really we are too earthly, too limited, we just have not got the capacity to love and trust ourselves to God who, as we learnt in our childhood, "is the Supreme Spirit who alone exists of himself and is infinite in all perfection". God whom we cannot visualize, cannot touch, cannot imagine, cannot know with our senses or with our tiny minds. God whom we could not love, but for one thing, one supreme mercy—this, that Christ has given us his own heart to love him with, his own mind to know him with, his own will to surrender ourselves to him with, and to put those whom we love into his hands, his hands of infinite mercy.

It is Christ in us who can say with absolute trust in the hour of death, "Under me are the everlasting arms".

It is Christ in us, Christ whose death we are dying, who can say with absolute faith, both for ourselves and for those whom we love, "Into thy hands, O Lord . . ."

That is why Christ would not, could not, come down from the Cross. On the Cross he carried us all through the darkness of death to the light, through the chill of death to the warmth, through the fear of death to the love of God. It is with his heart that we love the Father in the hour of death; because he has given his heart, he has given us our Heaven.

We are not alone in the hour of death. We have nothing to fear in the hour of death, because when the time comes Christ identifies himself with us so closely that fear gives way to trust and anguish to peace. He has lived all of our lives, died all of our deaths, to all of us he has given his peace.

It is in the hour of death that our fear, our anxiety, our loneliness, will end and we will understand Christ's words: "Peace is my bequest to you, and the peace which I give you is mine to give; I do not give peace as the world gives it. Do not let your heart be distressed, or play the coward" (John xiv. 27).

As Christ died on the Cross he drew all those to himself who would die his death and enter with him into the mysterious glory of it, all those who by dying would redeem other men—those whose lives seem to be failures, to be cut off before they have come to their flowering; those people who could have had brilliant careers, who could have benefited their fellow men immeasurably, but are cut off at the very beginning of manhood, or who die in childhood—deaths that seem to be nothing else but waste to which we cannot reconcile our hearts.

He identifies himself with all the young men who would die in battle, all the men and women who would fall in the squander of destruction that is war, all those children who would die in innocence with the burning splendour of *his* purity still radiant in their souls, with his passion of love still whole and not frittered away.

He identifies himself with the old people who, when death comes, will think their lives were wasted, who will think that they have done nothing for God's glory, taken no part in the world's redemption, but who in reality are dying his death and saving the world in the power of his love.

Christ on the Cross is God and man; he is wholly human, he knows the utter desolation and loneliness of death as no other man will ever know it. He knows the grief of leaving those whom he loves, his Mother, his friends, Mary Magdalene who seems utterly dependent on him.

He feels abandoned by his Father.

He is dying all our deaths. Death is too big a thing for any one of *us* to face alone. It separates us for a time from those we love on earth. It is difficult for us earth-bound, rooted creatures to want Heaven; it is impossible for us to realize what the glory of God will be to us. It is loving God, and that only, that can make Heaven Heaven. Here, imagination does not help us; we cannot really imagine ourselves loving the "Supreme Spirit"— we even *want* to cling to our human frailties and comforts, to our human weakness.

It is now that Christ takes over. He has died all our deaths on the Cross; now we are going to die his; it is Christ in us who surrenders to God. It is not with our own heart and our own will that we can long for God, but with Christ's. And Christ has given his heart and will to us. In this is the supreme mercy that comes to us in the hour of death.

"Father, into thy hands . . ." We can say it with Christ's love and trust in the Father. "Father, into thy hands not only my spirit, my body and soul, but those people whom I love, and whom you love infinitely more than I do."

Now I love God with Christ's will, with Christ's heart, with Christ's trust, and because he has taken possession of me, in the hour of my death I shall at least love my friends too with his love.

Not only will my suffering of mind and body, molten into his in the fire of his love, be the beginning of my blessed purgatory purifying me; it will also be Christ's sacrifice on the Cross offered for those whom I love.

Of each one surrendered wholly to Christ in the hour of death, we can say "Greater love than this no man has, that he lays down his life for his friends".

Prayer

"Father, into thy hands I commend my spirit!"
And into your hands, Jesus Christ,
my most merciful Redeemer,
Infinite Love,
I commend myself in the hour of death:
my body and soul,
my heart and my mind and my will,
all that I have, and all that I am.

Into your hands,
the beautiful hands of a carpenter
with their lines and sinew and muscle,
strong and sensitive hands
nailed to the Cross,
I commend those whom I love.
Hands that can heal the sick,
can give sight to the blind,
hands that can raise the dead
and restore them to life with a touch,
receive those whom I love
receive them and bless them from the Cross:
receive them, comfort them, lead and uphold them,
unite them to yourself
and re-unite them to me
for evermore in your Kingdom,
Jesus, merciful Lord.

THE THIRTEENTH STATION: JESUS IS TAKEN DOWN FROM THE CROSS

WHILE the soldiers divided Christ's garments among them and cast lots for his seamless cloak, Mary his Mother, she who had woven that beautiful cloak "from the top throughout", came with other holy women and stood at the foot of the Cross.

"So it was, then, that the soldiers occupied themselves; and . . . Mary the wife of Cleophas, and Mary Magdalene, had taken their stand beside the cross of Jesus" (John xix. 24–5).

She had followed him through the narrow streets of Jerusalem as one of the crowd; he did not speak to her in the crowd as he did to the women who wept over him, neither did he then give her a visible sign of his love as he did to St. Veronica when he imprinted her veil with the impression of his beautiful suffering face.

Even now she is mentioned only as one of a group of women who followed him, and there is nothing that she can do to alleviate his suffering. She is content to suffer with him; his Passion is hers.

How often before she has been one of the crowd! On the night of his birth she was one of the crowd thronging the little city of Bethlehem. When he was twelve years old she sought for him, lost, in the crowded city of Jerusalem, and when she found him in the temple she heard that strange puzzling answer of his to her

question, "My son, why hast thou treated us so?
Think what anguish of mind thy father and I have
endured searching for thee. But he asked them, What
reason had you to search for me? Could you not tell
that I must needs be in the place which belongs to my
Father? These words which he spoke to them were
beyond their understanding. . . ."

Again, Mary his Mother was in the crowd when
her son was preaching and, again, what he said
would have baffled any mother whose love was less
perfect than hers, one who had less understanding of
her son than she had of Jesus, and who was less
identified with him in his every desire, in every beat
of his heart.

"While he was still speaking to the multitude, it
chanced that his Mother and brethren were standing
without, desiring speech with him. And someone told
him, Here are thy mother and thy brethren standing
without, looking for thee. But he made answer to the
man that brought him the news, Who is a mother, who
are brethren to me? Then he stretched out his hand
towards his disciples, and said, Here are my mother
and my brethren! If any one does the will of my Father
who is heaven, he is my brother, and sister, and
mother."

She was surely in the crowd when Christ rode into
Jerusalem on the proud little donkey and the children
cast their garments and the branches from the trees
under its feet; and, so soon after, in the midst of the
mob that cried out, "Crucify him"; and again on the
way to Calvary following him, longing to take some of
the load of the great Cross, but by his own will denied
the comfort of helping or comforting him, because she

was absolutely one with him and she only in the whole world could enter into his Passion and suffer *everything* that he suffered with him.

Now at the end she is still in the crowd that mills around the foot of the Cross—the soldiers, the mockers, the curious, and a handful of those who in spite of everything are faithful to him: and surely a multitude of those who heard his Sermon on the Mount and hoped, but who have lost hope now and feel themselves cheated; those who could not dream of the glory that is coming to them and to all who will open their hearts to him, his resurrection in their hearts, his rebirth in their souls!

Only Jesus and Mary know how like this night is to that one in the little city of Bethlehem thirty-three years ago—that night when she heard the first cry of her little son.

That was a little wail, no stronger than the bleating of one of the lambs on the hillside, bleating in the darkness of the night; this cry from the Cross was a loud cry, uttered again in darkness: "Then Jesus cried out again in a loud voice, and yielded up his spirit" (Matt. xxvii. 50).

Mary remained silent, as so often before she had remained silent in the crowd; but now Jesus shared her silence. Jesus and Mary alone were silent in the midst of chaos, when the veil of the temple was rent from top to bottom and the graves were opened; they alone remained calm when those who, a few moments ago, had mocked at Christ, and those who had hammered the nails through his hands and feet, shouting and laughing to one another, were seized with dread and confusion of mind.

One of the soldiers came to pierce the heart of Christ with a spear, and as he drove it into his side, blood and water flowed from it. Mary knew that that stream of blood was her own blood, emptied at last from his sacred veins, and she knew that that water that sprang like the spray of a fountain from his side, was the mysterious breaking of the waters of birth. It was the birth of Christ in man—her son Christ who would indwell men until the end of time.

They took his body down from the Cross and laid it in his Mother's arms, and she held it upon her heart and, in it, all those Christs to come, to whom she was Mother now.

That first birth of Christ in Bethlehem was painless because Mary his Mother was sinless and he was the Son of God. But this mysterious birth of Christ on Calvary began in the travail and agony of the whole world borne by one man and one woman—God made man, and Mary his Mother—because this was the birth of Christ in us, Christ the Redeemer born in the souls of sinners; and every sinner who would receive him in all time became Mary's child, even her only child; every sinner who would be indwelt by Christ was laid in Mary's arms, and she received them all.

Mankind was born again.

Already, even in the agony of that night of sorrow, Mary, who had shared Christ's Passion, shared his peace. In the consummation of his pain, and her pain and suffering, she knew the beginning of the joy that would never end; she knew the birth of life in the souls of men, that would be *immortal* life, never ending. She knew the utter joy of experiencing the consummation of *his* love for men, and of loving them with all *his* love.

She herself was indwelt by him now as really as her body had been indwelt by his advent. Now she who had given him life would live his life for ever, her life would be his, her words his words, her acts his acts, her heart beating, the beating of his heart.

She who had said long ago in Nazareth, "Let it be unto me according to thy word" (Luke i. 38), was the first of all human creatures since Christ was conceived to be one with him; she gave him her life and he gave her back her life in his for ever. He gave his life too, to all those who would receive him through the ages— "And I have given them the privilege which thou gavest to me—that they should all be one, as we are one; that while thou art in me, I may be in them and so they may be perfectly made one" (John xvii. 22–3).

As the dead Christ lay in his Mother's arms, she laid to her heart all those sinners to whom he would give, not only life, but his *own* life. In baptism, that first stream of the waters of birth, cleansing and irrigating the soul; in the sacrament of penance, restoring the soul of the sinner to its primal innocence. She saw them as God sees them; no matter how battered and bruised they had been by sin, the innocence of Christ was restored to them, they were restored to his beauty. No matter how darkened their minds and hearts had been by evil, and by the oppressive sadness that follows upon evil, they shone now with the purity, the glory of Christ on Tabor, clothed in his loveliness that burns with the splendour of a fire of snow. No matter how cynical and faded and old their sins had made them, they were restored to their childhood now, to Christ's childhood; now they could possess the Kingdom of Heaven in a wild flower, a stream of water or a star; and now in the Body of Christ Mary took them, each of them as her only child, to her sinless heart.

And there from the summit of Calvary, at the foot of the Cross, with her dead child in her arms, Mary saw how in all the centuries to come Christ would be born again day after day, hour after hour, in the Sacred Host. She heard the multitudinous whisper of the words of Consecration coming to her on Calvary from every part of the world, from every place on earth, from the great cathedrals of the world, from the little village huts that are makeshift for churches, from the churches themselves, whether they were beautiful or cheap and tawdry—from the chapels and wards of hospitals, from prisons and from concentration camps, from the frozen forests of Siberia. From dawn till dusk, and from dusk till dawn, the words of Consecration on the breath of men, and Jesus lifted up, as he had been lifted up on the Cross, in the Sacred Host.

And she saw through the darkness that covered Calvary how, at all those Masses, those who were to be her children and the children of God, would flock to the altars to receive her son in the Host—little children clothed in the white muslin and gossamer of their First Communion clothes, old people leaning upon their sticks, young men and women who would carry Christ in their hearts to face and conquer the work-a-day world.

She saw, too, how he would be carried into prisons and hospitals and concentration camps, to be given to the lonely and the sick and the dying. And how in all these people, in every one of them, sinners as well as saints, Christ her son would live again and overcome the world.

So it was that when Jesus was taken down from the Cross, Mary received her dead son into her arms and took the whole world to her heart.

Prayer

Mary, Mother of God,
receiving the dead body
of Jesus Christ your son,
taken down from the Cross
and laid in your arms—
receive us
to whom he has given his life
and lay us with him
and in him
upon your sinless heart.

We are sinners,
but save us from despondency
and despair,
save us from morbidity
which kills the soul,
save us from dwelling on the past.
Take our heads into your hands
and turn them gently
to look upon the light of God.
Let us feel the warmth and radiance
of that healing sun,
although we are still too weak
to bear the blaze of its glory.

By the dead body of Christ
laid in your arms,
save us from the death of sin,
ask our Heavenly Father
whose will is your will

to restore us to life,
to Christ's life in our souls,
so that in each one of us
you may see your only child,
the child Jesus,
and give us the Heaven
of your tender love.

By the Passion
and Death
of your only son,
give us his life—
make us new,
give us the trust
of children,
give us the childhood of Christ,
grant to us,
Virgin Mother,
a new Heaven and a new earth,
because we see with his eyes,
hear with his ears,
work with his hands,
walk on his feet,
trust with his trust
in his Heavenly Father,
and love with his heart.

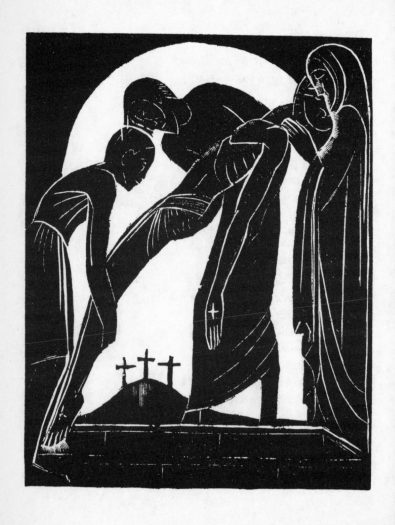

THE FOURTEENTH STATION: JESUS IS
LAID IN THE TOMB

THE BIRTH of Christ into this world was in one sense a parting from his Mother. It had to be so. Now he is lifted from her arms by his disciples and made ready for his burial.

His burial is like his birth. When he was born his Mother was in a strange city; she was not in Nazareth in the little home that she had prepared for him; she had with her some swaddling bands to wrap him in— the beautiful little garments she had been weaving for him were left at home. She did not know when she and Joseph set out for Bethlehem that years would pass before they could return, or that the wooden cradle that Joseph had made for him with such love and care, such scrupulous craftsmanship, would never be used by him—or that he must lie in a borrowed bed, a manger borrowed from humble animals, with a mattress of straw.

Mary must indeed have remembered that night now when, hurriedly, because all must be done before to-morrow's feast, Jesus was laid in a borrowed tomb. "In the quarter where he was crucified there was a garden with a new tomb in it, one in which no man had ever yet been buried. Here since the tomb was close at hand, they laid Jesus, because of the Jewish Feast on the morrow" (John xix. 41–2). Just as he came into the world with nothing of his own, it seems now that he will go out of it possessing nothing, not even his own garments, the garments that his Mother wove for him; not even his own resting place, his own tomb.

Again history repeats itself. When he was born, wise men came to Jesus bringing him myrrh and frankincense and gold, and offered them to him as he lay in his swaddling bands; and now Nicodemus comes with myrrh and aloes, and "they took Jesus' body then, and wrapped it in winding cloths with the spices".

So night fell; everything, it seemed, was over; the faithful apostle, Nicodemus, who lent him his tomb, and the holy women, could do no more. It was like the dreadful anti-climax that follows every funeral, every death. Everyone who had loved him was exhausted, emptied out. It seemed that the whole world was emptied out, that there was no longer any meaning or any purpose in anything.

Yet it would seem, looking back down the years, that there has never been a night so pregnant with life, so full of mercy and eternal love as that night, a night of *such* meaning and *such* purpose.

Christ was in the tomb; the whole world was sown with the seed of Christ's life; that which happened thirty years ago in the womb of the Virgin Mother was happening now, but now it was happening yet more secretly, yet more mysteriously, in the womb of the whole world.

Christ had already told those who flocked to hear him preach that the seed must fall into the earth, or else remain by itself alone; now the seed of his life was hidden in darkness in order that his life should quicken in countless hearts over and over again for all time.

His burial which seemed to be the end was the beginning, it was the beginning of Christ-life in multitudes of souls; it was the beginning, too, of the *renewal* of Christ's life in countless souls.

For just as Christ was soon to rise from the dead with his human body and live again on earth, he would rise from the dead over and over again in a spiritual sense, in the souls of countless sinners everywhere until the end of time.

From that hour for as long as the world lasted there would be resurrection everywhere. Christ-life would return to souls of sinners who wept for their sins, as spring returns in all its loveliness of delicate grass and wild flower to the dark hard earth watered by the rain of April.

On the night of Christ's burial, many who loved him must have been overwhelmed by grief and exhaustion that threatened to become despair, yet never has there been a night in the whole history of mankind so pregnant with the secret of the unending life and joy that was to break upon the world with the dawn.

For Christ himself, pain and suffering had ended. Only in his members, those "other Christs" in whom his life on earth would go on through time, would he suffer any more. Their suffering would be transformed into his; and never could it be for them, no matter how terrible it might sometimes seem to be, the complete agony, the absolute darkness, that it was for him in his human life, because not only would Christ have already experienced everything they would do, but he would have already overcome all those things they feared—"Fear not," he had said to his apostles, and to all who would follow him in all time, "Fear not, for I have overcome the world." As if he would say to each and every one of us whom he would indwell, "Fear not, for I have overcome your sins, I have overcome your temptations, I have overcome all things that you shrink from, all your sufferings of mind and body. Fear not, for I am within you, I who have already overcome the world."

Jesus lying in the borrowed tomb was at peace—his suffering was over, his love was consummated, every hour of darkness moved closer to the light, closer to the morning of resurrection, closer to the time when he would rise from the dead to live for ever.

In every life of every Christian there are countless resurrections—just as there are always many times when every Christian is buried with Christ.

In the soul of the sinner Christ dies many deaths and knows the glory of many resurrections.

In the souls that have served him faithfully, too, there are long periods that seem like death: periods of dryness of spirit, when all the spiritual things that once interested them have become insufferably tedious and boring, when it is very difficult, even sometimes impossible, to say a prayer. When the sweetness has gone out of the love of God, when the soul seems bound in the iron bondage of the winter of the spirit, like the seed held in the iron of the black frozen earth in the winter time.

These are the winters of the spirit indeed! But just as Christ suffered everything that all those who were to follow him would suffer, all those "other Christs" who have come after him have suffered, and will suffer in a spiritual sense, everything that he suffered in his human life on earth.

One of these things is lying in the tomb, bound and restricted in the burial bands. There come times in every life when the soul seems to be shut down, frost-bound in the hard, iron-bound winter of the spirit. Times when it seems to be impossible to pray, impossible even to want to pray, when there seems to be only cold and darkness numbing the mind.

These indeed are the times when Christ is growing towards his flowering, towards his spring breaking in the soul. Towards his ever-recurring resurrection in the world. Towards his glorious resurrection in the hearts of men.

Again and again he has referred to himself and to his divine life in us, as seed buried in the earth, and so it is. There are times when we experience no sweetness, no consolation, no visible sign of the presence and the growth of Christ in us; these above all other times are those in which Christ does in fact grow to his flowering in us.

There seems to be nothing that we can do in these times to honour God, but by ourselves there is nothing that we can do at *any* time.

In Christ we can do just what he did, remain quietly in the tomb, rest and be at peace, trusting God to awaken us in his own good time to a springtime of Christ, to a sudden quickening and flowering and new realization of Christ-life in us.

It is always from the deaths of the spirit that Christ's resurrection comes. When we know ourselves as sinners and are sorry, our resurrection is at hand. When we are iron-bound in the winter frost of aridity, the springtide of resurrection is very near.

When it seems that we have failed, that everything is over, and we are in the darkness of the tomb with

Christ, then the angels will come and roll away the great heavy stone, and resurrection with Christ will come.

There are many deaths before the death of the body; there are many, many resurrections before that last eternal resurrection that will re-unite our bodies and souls for ever, to live for ever full lives of love and end- less bliss, that will never be interrupted again.

All these little deaths of the spirit show us the mystery of that last death, and that endless rising from the dead.

Death is not something to fear. Fear will be over and done with when it comes. Then the possibility of sin will be over, the danger of ever again being parted from Christ will be over, the pains and the desolations of body and soul on earth will be over.

We will not be parted from those whom we love on earth, but only hidden from them for a time—a time that will pass swiftly and, when it is past, we will be re-united with everyone we loved here for ever, with no more fear of loss, with no shadow at all cast upon our human love.

We have nothing to fear.

Christ has died each of our deaths for us. He will be with us all, saint and sinner alike, in our rising from the dead.

It is to each one of us that he spoke on the night before he died, saying, "Peace is my bequest to you, and the peace which I give you is mine to give; I do not give peace as the world gives it. Do not let your heart be distressed or play the coward" (John xiv. 27).

So be it—Come! Lord Jesus, come! "Into your hands I commit my spirit."

Prayer

Jesus
buried in the tomb,
Jesus in burial bands,
you are life
and the source of life;
you are the seed in the earth,
the secret of the Eternal Spring;
you are the wonder of Heaven
and love's unending flowering.

Let us,
poor sinners,
die and be buried with you
and so
rise with you
in your glory.

Grant to us all,
Lord Jesus,
that in the soul's long winters
we may wait patiently,
grow imperceptibly,
in the rhythms and seasons
of your love
and so enter into your peace.

Give us grace
to wait patiently,
without doubt,
without impatience,

without anxiety,
for the morning of resurrection.

May every little death in life
teach us how to die
the last death
that is the beginning
of true life.
Be our life to us
on earth, Lord Jesus,
and our Everlasting Life.

Lord Jesus,
today,
we accept
from your merciful hands
what is to come.
The times of trial in this world,
the suffering of our death,
the sorrow and loneliness
of our last hours upon earth,
the purifying,
unknown pains of our purgatory.

Into your hands, O Lord,
into your hands,
we commit our living and dying,
knowing
that you are
the dawn of eternal day,
the burning light of the morning star.